Cultural Change and Identity

Cultural Change and Identity:

Mandailing Immigrants in West Malaysia

DONALD TUGBY

University of Queensland Press

© University of Queensland Press,
St. Lucia, Queensland, 1977

Typeset, printed and bound by Academy Press Pty. Ltd., Brisbane

Distributed in the United Kingdom, Europe, the Middle East, Africa, and the Caribbean by Prentice-Hall International, International Book Distributors Ltd., 66 Wood Lane End, Hemel Hempstead, Herts., England

*National Library of Australia
Cataloguing-in-publication data*

Tugby, Donald John, 1920–.
    Cultural change and identity.

    Index.
    Bibliography.
    ISBN 0 7022 1361 6.

    1. Batak – Social life and customs. I. Title.

301.295951

To my parents

Contents

Illustrations

FIGURES

MAPS

Acknowledgments

Professor Michael Swift of Monash University, Melbourne told the author about a Mandailing community in Negeri Sembilan and thus provided a starting point for the fieldwork. The author's initiation in Malaysia was eased by sound advice from Tan Sri Mubin Sheppard.

Many Malaysian officials generously gave help during the fieldwork, especially the district officers, assistant district officers, *Penghulu*, and village heads in the areas visited. Help was also forthcoming from the academic community in Malaysia and especially from the members of the Department of Malay Studies and the Department of Geography at the University of Malaya and the Department of History at the National University. The help given by Mrs. Fan Kok-Sim and the staff of the Reference Section, University of Malaya Library was more than any visiting scholar could hope for. Much of this work could never have been completed but for the ready help and insightful advice given by Professor Ungku Aziz, vice-chancellor of the University of Malaya, to whom the author is especially grateful.

The maps were drawn by the ever patient Eric Savage, cartographer in the Department of Geography, University of Queensland, and the index was prepared by Dianne Hungerford. Finally the author wishes to thank his wife, Dr. Elise Tugby, who helped him in the field in 1973 and with the maps.

The source for place names on the maps is the map Malaysia Barat 1967 published by the Directorate of Mapping, Malaysia, Sheets 1 and 2.

The financial support given to the study by the Australian Research Grants Committee and the Research Committee of the University of Queensland is gratefully acknowledged.

Introduction

This study is about cultural change among Mandailing immigrants in West Malaysia. The author worked in the Mandailing homeland in the extreme southern part of the Tapanuli area in North Sumatra in 1955-56, and got to know the Mandailing people well. But he could not understand to his satisfaction how the Batak style of political and social system functioned among the Islamic Mandailingers. That system was not working in the villages as it had before World War II because the indigenous political heads were not restored after the Indonesian Revolution. When the author heard that in Malaya there were long-established Mandailing communities he went there in 1962 hoping to find the pre-World War II social and political system still functioning in a Mandailing community. Because Malaya achieved Independence without revolution it was hoped that the pre-World War II socio-political system might have survived intact. The search extended through thirty-two Mandailing communities in the western part of West Malaysia, but nowhere had the pre-World War II socio-political system survived. A new problem arose. The Mandailing migrants had lost the culture they brought with them from Sumatra to varying degrees ... how had this happened? A more systematic survey was made in 1968 in an attempt to answer this question, brief visits to Malaysia were made in 1971 and 1972, and in late 1973 and early 1974 most of the communities were revisited. Data on cultural change in these communities over a period of fifteen years have therefore been gathered.

After the initial field visit to Malaysia the following question arose: if the Mandailingers in Malaya were not "proper" Mandailingers, culturally speaking, what were they? Had they become in varying degrees "Malays"? To answer this question a clear idea of "Malay" culture was needed. Accordingly, an attempt was made to build from library sources a model of "Malay" culture in order to provide a yardstick for measuring the degree to which each Mandailing community had adopted "Malay" culture. This effort proved hopeless. It became obvious that the "Real Malay" or any ethnographer's "Malay" is a patchwork created by bringing together snippets from culturally diverse sources in Kelantan, Johore, Kedah, Negeri Sembilan, Singapore, Trengganu and Petani.

It was therefore decided to measure the loss of Mandailing cultural features in Mandailing communities in Malaya and to relaté this loss to other features of the social and economic history and contemporary social and economic situation in those communities. A questionnaire covering the main elements of Mandailing culture was built up on the basis of previous field experience in the Mandailing homeland. During group interviews in each village in Malaysia questions were also asked about the history, economic composition, and functioning of the village in an attempt to identify the features associated with the loss of Mandailing culture. Some cultural changes originated in compromises made willingly by the villagers, some arose from economic compulsion (such as the spread of tin mining), and some were brought about by the activities of the government, especially in rural development. It was found that the degree to which Mandailing culture was retained was most strongly associated with the type of subsistence base (wet rice or rubber production) and the percentage of Mandailing families in the village community as a whole.

This study is divided into two parts. The first deals with the cultural loss and replacement that have taken place as the Mandailingers in West Malaysia have adapted themselves to different local conditions; the second deals with changes in attitudes and identity brought about by the nation-building efforts of the Malaysian government. As a part of those efforts the government has promoted a programme of rural development whose political aim was to retain for the government the consolidated support of the mainly rural-dwelling Malays. In implementing this programme no distinction has been drawn between indigenous Malays and Sumatran and other immigrants from Indonesia. The latter are subsumed under the programme as "Malays" and are therefore encouraged to accept this beneficial identity. It is this process of identity change that the author believes can be properly called "Malayanization".[1]

During the course of the study it became clear that the Mandailingers in West Malaysia retain the economic orientation and pragmatism characteristic of the Mandailingers in the Sumatran homeland. They stay where they are because they think they can do better for themselves there at the moment. On their part identity is determined by political and economic convenience; hence the title of this book.

PART ONE

PART ONE

1
The Malaysian context

The Straits of Malacca have never been a formidable barrier to human movement from Malaysia to Sumatra or vice versa. They are only wide at Malacca and south of Singapore it is possible to get across by hopping from island to island. The weather in the Straits is never very stormy and the currents are not severe, but there are some shoals off the west coast of Malaya.[1] The cross-Straits traffic is intersected by larger ships which to take the shortest sea route from India to China must travel through the Straits past the southward thrusting peninsula of West Malaysia. To gain control of this important seaway from one side, or better from both sides at once, has been part of the strategy of empire-building in the Straits region.[2] The conjunction of foreign trading vessels and local shipping has led these trade-based powers to be centred on an emporium port such as Malacca. By attracting migrants with new ideas, these ports have acted as important centres of economic development, social change, and cultural diffusion.[3]

The entry of the Europeans into the area was a phase in this process. The European incursion stopped local powers spanning the Straits and by control of the seas reduced piracy and military excursions. By monopolistic practices and the founding of new ports the Europeans undermined the economic basis for expansion by local powers.[4] But piracy did not cease; indeed local powers, robbed of their opportunities for empire-building and frustrated economically, indulged in it.[5] The pirates' challenge to European seapower was not overcome until the Europeans asserted their technical superiority in ships in the period 1837-50. From this time onwards European ideas about economic development, law, and administration became dominant.

The nineteenth century was a period of rapid economic redevelopment in an atmosphere of comparative political stability. After the Treaty of London the British took over the role of dominant maritime power in the Straits, while from their base in Java the

Dutch began slowly to extend their control over Sumatra by seizing whatever opportunities came their way for penetration into the interior. From the point of view of this account of Mandailing migration the most important occurrence of this kind was during the Paderi wars when the Dutch were asked by the Mandailing *rajas* for help against the Paderis and sent troops into the interior.[6] After the war Dutch administrative posts were set up in Mandailing and the Dutch began a new phase in the process of colonization including demands for labour and the production of more cash crops. The economic disruption caused by the war no doubt stimulated movements of people within and out of Mandailing and Mandailing migration to Malaya may have started in this period. At the same time events in Malaya became focussed upon internal economic development which reached a scale beyond the power of control of indigenous political institutions. I shall now deal with economic development and political stability in the various regions of Malaya in the period 1824-76 in so far as they affected intending migrants.

Malayan ecosystems 1824-76: a geographical overview

Kedah, Perlis, and Penang (see map 1)

The indigenous population and economy of Kedah and Perlis grew slowly from the establishment of Indianized settlement at the river mouths in the fifth century. A spurt in population took place at that time and again as wet-rice growing spread in the fourteenth century. Economic development was dominated by the spread of subsistence wet-rice growing into the foothill zones, the central swamps and finally, by virtue of canal building towards the end of the nineteenth century, the coastal swamps. As new areas became available they were occupied by local peasant farmers.[7] There was little economic opportunity for immigrants.[8]

Moreover immigration was discouraged by political events. Kedah was under Thai suzereignty for the whole of the nineteenth century. In 1818 Kedah was ordered by Thailand to attack Perak. In 1824 she was herself invaded by Thailand and half the population, including the sultan, fled to Province Wellesley, which had been ceded to the British in 1800. Repeated attempts were made to drive the Thai out but the sultan was able to return to his throne in 1842

Map 1 Western States of West Malaysia

only on Thai terms. Thereafter the indigenous population returned, Thai control ameliorated, and from 1860 political refugees from Acheh, but no other Sumatrans, entered the state. The population of Kedah was estimated to be 50,000 at the beginning of the nineteenth century and at the end of it 219,000.[9]

Stable conditions with economic opportunities attracted Chinese and Indian settlers to Penang and encouraged Malays to move from Kedah to nearby Province Wellesley. In 1801 the population was about 15,000; in 1901 about 244,000. The percentage of Malays, Chinese, Indians, and others in 1833 was 68.4, 12.8, 12.0, and 6.8 respectively and in 1901, 42.3, 39.9, 15.5, and 2.3 respectively. Most of the Chinese and Indian immigrants went to Penang. Thus potential Sumatran migrants faced heavy competition from Chinese and Indians if they went as traders to Penang and from established Kedah migrants if they went as farmers to Province Wellesley.

Perak and Selangor

The west coast states of Perak and Selangor have substantial mountain zones in their eastern part, a broad tin-bearing foothill zone, and a coastal plain of gentle slope, subject to flooding. These states are dissected by the Perak, Bernam, Selangor and Langat rivers and other streams which flow south from their mountain sources and then westwards across the plain. The rivers and streams were the critical geographic features in the nineteenth century. They acted as avenues of communication; they were a means of transport; they provided water for wet-rice growing and tin mining; and they were the sites of alluvial tin and gold. The jungle-clad watersheds were occupied by Aborigines; the Malay villages were along the river banks or along the coastal dunes out of reach of the tide.

The major settlements were at trans-shipment points near the river mouths, and out of reach of flood. Each inland chief controlled a section of the river and was able to exact tolls on downward moving produce and upward moving provisions. This situation persisted at least until the 1880s owing to the unwillingness of local chiefs to give up their prerogatives, although in the meantime the economy was revolutionized and the population pattern grossly changed.

The dominant event of the nineteenth century from the social and economic point of view was the development of large-scale tin mining by immigrant Chinese. The west coast states at the beginning of the nineteenth century exported small quantities of pepper, cloves, hides, gutta percha, rattan, and tin, and imported cloth, salt, and rice. The Malays produced tin by the *lampan* method which required a relatively small labour unit.[10] Miners from Sumatra could work tin or seek for gold. But during the first half of the nineteenth century the demand for tin in Europe outstripped the local supply. Malayan tin which until 1850 had found its main market in India and China was now in demand in Europe. Exploration parties entered the foothill zone and major mining areas were successively opened in Sungai Ujong, Lukut, and the upper Kelang valley. In Perak, tin mining was largely confined to small areas in Batang Padang, Lower Perak, and around Bidor until 1848 when the richer deposits of Larut were found.[11] The initiative in these developments was sometimes taken by Sumatran miners and sometimes by local leaders, but most of the larger-scale ventures were organized by Chinese leaders using imported Chinese indentured labour and working with local Malay chiefs backed by Chinese financiers and secret society leaders in Penang, Malacca, and Singapore.[12] There were, however, some exceptions. In the 1870s the sultan of Perak "threatened to kill one Kulop Riau for having built a road and imported a few hundred Mendelings from Sumatra to open mines at Sungai Raya, because, he said, roads and mines attracted Europeans ... "[13]

The Malay political and social setting in which these developments took place was feudal in form. In Perak there was a hierarchy of titleholders; four of the first rank, eight of the second, and sixteen of the third who functioned as territorial chiefs. The sultan had to consult the chiefs and *waris negeri*[14] on matters of state. In Selangor there was no established hierarchy of title holders and districts were governed by members of the royal household. The *raja* had rights over unused land and could exact forced labour or drive men and their families into debt bondage. The well-being, even the life, of the commoner was in the hands of the *raja*.

Squabbles about succession to office which led to civil war reduced the social and economic security of the common man still further. In the period of the tin boom these squabbles were exacerbated by the difference in the productivity of different regions and by quarrels between rival Chinese secret societies which were beyond the power of control of regional chiefs.[15] The Selangor civil war of

1870-73 and the breakdown of administration in Perak owing to a quarrel over succession to the sultanship in 1871 were the culminating events of this phase of disruption. Rivalry between groups of non-Chinese miners was revealed in the course of events: "Sumatran Mendiling from Batu Bahara" and Bugis settlers, both of whom were living in a tin-mining village near Simpang in 1866, fought each other for several months, ostensibly in support of the rival sides in the Selangor civil war, without intervention by the local Malays.[16]

Negeri Sembilan

The expansion of tin production in the nineteenth century disrupted the Negeri Sembilan polity but did not lead to a new pattern of land occupation and population. There were about six hundred Chinese miners in Sungai Ujong in 1828 and Malays and Chinese were mining tin and gold at Gemencheh. The main export route for tin was through the valley of the river Linggi. Rivalry among the chiefs who exacted tolls along the route increased as production expanded. Economic competition between local chiefs and squabbles between Sumatran (Menangkabau) and local claimants to high state offices led to the disintegration of the Negeri Sembilan state which had emerged with the importation of a paramount ruler from Sumatra in 1773. Some farmers were forced from the fields by short wars. In Jelebu half the population emigrated to other states in the period 1860 to 1880.[17] Although Sungai Ujong accepted protection in 1874 it was not until after 1886 when the other states followed suit that European administration was effectively introduced. But the long-established matrilineally organized social system within each petty state, so different from corresponding institutions elsewhere in Malaya, remained intact. Malay immigrants could not compromise with it; they could only allow themselves to be absorbed by it. Hence a composite Malay society was not formed.

Malacca declined under the Dutch and at the end of the eighteenth century its population was only 1,500. It recovered in the nineteenth century under the British and became, apart from its function as an entrepot port, a centre for Chinese financiers. Immigrant peasant farmers did not settle there.

Johore

The division of the Johore empire under the treaty of 1824 left the more populous part based on Riau under Dutch control and the almost uninhabited part, the southern portion of the Malaysian peninsula, under the influence of the British in Singapore. A dispute between claimants to the sultanship was settled by granting one of the claimants a pension and the state settled down to a steady growth of revenue. Chinese pepper and gambier planters moved in on the west side but, as there was no significant development of tin mining, the economic conditions were not attractive to Sumatran migrants.

Singapore developed rapidly as a trading centre after its foundation in 1819 and by 1862 had a population of 90,000, mainly Chinese, but including also Indians and Indonesians. A small community of Bataks from Sumatra were growing rice in Paya Lebar in 1849.[18]

The east coast

The political system and social conditions in Pahang, Trengganu, and Kelantan in the eighteenth century were similar to those in Perak prior to 1850 but these states were not disturbed by the development of large-scale mining, were not on the main trading route, and had little export trade. Nevertheless their future potential was of interest to the British; hence, when the Thai attempted to assert more strongly the suzereignty which they claimed over Kelantan and Trengganu and to make their own nominee sultan of Pahang, they were repulsed by a British gunboat at Kuala Trengganu in 1862.

The long-standing China trade offered some opportunity and there were Chinese settlements at the mouth of the Pahang river and at Kuala Trengganu, but no large-scale Chinese immigration took place. Pahang was disturbed by continued quarrels between the sultan and up-river chiefs which no doubt disrupted the economy, while Kelantan and Trengganu had long-established indigenous Malay communities in occupation of the best land. Hence, for a number of reasons—internecine strife, lack of economic opportunity, and uncertain political future—those states were not attractive to migrants. As far as the Mandailingers were concerned they were on the side of the Malay Peninsula remote from Sumatra and hence outside the Straits-based economic orbit and they did not have the tin-mining and ancillary trading activities which enabled a settler to meet his temporary needs and, in the longer run, fulfil his economic ambitions.

The exploitation of the environment, 1824-76

The economic development of Malaya in this period was a function of the concession-granting and taxation powers of the sultans and chiefs and the resources of the entrepreneurs.[19] The Chinese tin miners were backed by big financiers, and had a large supply of cheap indentured labour and good technological knowledge. They could operate on a large scale. The Indonesian migrants had less technical knowledge, an uncertain labour supply, and less financial backing. They were probably more mobile than the Chinese and gravitated in small groups towards the more easily won deposits. New Indonesian migrants joined kinsmen or members of their own culture group. Some immigrants worked on plantations and others produced food for the non-agriculturalists.

The indigenous positions of power in Malaya were ascribed, only limited power could be achieved by economic success and even to this immigrant Indonesians could rarely aspire because of their lack of resources. The best course for immigrants therefore was to identify themselves as Malays and seek the favour of a local leader.

In short, in the early part of the period from 1824 to 1876 the primary condition for attracting Mandailing migrants, i.e. the existence of economic opportunities, was well fulfilled in the foothill zones of Perak, Selangor, and Negeri Sembilan; but in the last the patrilineal Mandailingers were unwelcome. In the latter part of the period, the economic opportunities in tin mining disappeared because of heavy competition from the Chinese and civil strife.

The effects of British intervention

British intervention restored conditions under which the economy could expand and thereby stimulated immigration in the west coast states. Law and order were restored in Perak, Selangor, and Sungai Ujong under treaties concluded in 1874. Disturbances continued in Pahang until 1895 because there the chiefs recognized that the residential system would lead to the loss of their power. On the formation of the Federated Malay States comprised of Perak,

Selangor, Negeri Sembilan (now united), and Pahang in 1896 the chiefs did in fact lose their independence because the collection of revenue was under British control. The administration was now firmly in British hands and was used to create conditions for economic expansion, especially in Perak and Selangor. Kedah, Perlis, Kelantan and Trengganu remained under Thai suzereignty until 1909 when British advisers were appointed. An official adviser was appointed in Johore in 1914. The five unfederated Malay states each relied upon its own revenue. Kedah and Johore benefited from association with nearby trading centres but Kelantan and Trengganu remained undeveloped and traditionally Malay in character.

Although there were some rapid political settlements, and some rather slower administrative changes, in the western states south of Kedah after intervention the economy took the same course as in the 1860s, i.e. continuous expansion of tin mining with breakouts of boom conditions locally. Relatively large-scale movements of population into and around the country took place. However an accentuation of the regional differences already mentioned and some specific legislation on land tenure made some regions more attractive to migrants than others. I shall now deal with these matters.

Development under British influence 1876-1946

Early land policy

The land policy adopted under British influence made the Federated Malay States attractive to new settlers and agricultural enterprises. The land tenure system used in Perak and Selangor before 1874 was probably based on that of Malacca.[20] The indigenous Malay peasant had usufructuary rights over unused land. He could clear virgin forest or secondary forest which had grown up on abandoned plots and make use of the land. If he continued to use the land he gained a proprietary right over it. If the land was abandoned it reverted to the pool of land available for use. Wet-rice land was deemed to be abandoned when it had not been used for three seasons, but orchards not until the trees were no longer visible. These rights became subject to the payment of a tithe of one-tenth of the annual produce to the sultan when the latter came to be regarded as the religious head of the state. Moreover the sultan had rights of disposal over wasteland. These rights he could transfer without loss of ultimate control to a nominee such as a court favourite, kinsman, local chief, or, in the case of right to receive tithes, to a collector. As the sultan or his nominee had discretionary powers in the exercise of these rights, especially in determining the proportion of the crop to be paid as tithe, the peasant proprietor had little economic security. He could protect himself only by becoming a kinsman or client of a local chief. Permanent settlers could not be easily attracted under these conditions.

Under British influence new systems of land tenure were introduced although a uniform code for Perak, Selangor, Negeri Sembilan, and Pahang was not achieved until 1897. The General Land Regulations issued in Perak in 1879 recognized Malay tenure for land already occupied but called for the terms of tenure to be superseded by a 999-year lease after survey. Other types of British land tenure and land classes were introduced in the codes promulgated for different areas and states. The lack of uniformity in regulations was no deterrent to settlers who occupied land at a pace in advance of the capacity of the administration to undertake survey and registration. Occupation without title was therefore common.

The keynote of British policy was economic development under control. In the compromise land code of 1897 Malay land was recognized and periodic reassessment of rent was provided for so that the state could share in any increase in prosperity. But in the implementation of this and the previous codes principles of tenure gave way before economic necessity—the squatters in effect exercised the old indigenous Malay usufructuary right, but had to yield before the demands of the large-scale mining enterprises. Thus in the foothill zone of Perak and Selangor the pioneers on the fringe of settlement had constantly to move on as the mines advanced or adjust to an ecosystem which could no longer support wet-rice cultivation. Thus were initiated the differences in the mode of subsistence that distinguish one type of immigrant village from another.

Tin, rubber, and rice

The export tax on tin was the most important source of revenue for development needs such as roads and railways. The British encouraged the Chinese to expand production and by 1899 Malaya produced more than 44,000 tonnes or 53.1 per cent of the world total, mainly from Chinese-owned mines.[21] Production by Malays was comparatively insignificant. The industry received a further fillip when British and other foreign capital flowed in in the early years of the twentieth century. The dredge, introduced in 1913, increased the amount of capital required and with other technological improvements halved the labour used in the industry, thus releasing many Chinese workers. The price for tin varied markedly with world demand. Tin mining was not for the small-scale Malay producer a profitable full-time occupation in this period.

Rubber growing on the other hand was well adapted to the needs of Malay and immigrant Indonesian peasant farmers and by 1900 it was clear that there was no future in coffee.[22] The area under plantation rubber expanded rapidly as world demand increased in the early years of the twentieth century and smallholders became interested. The peak prices were in the 1910-12 period when many Malays turned their rice fields into rubber gardens. Plots of unused land were also readily available under the liberal land policy so that a new migrant, provided he could sustain himself during the growing period of the rubber trees, could become well established in about ten years.

Chinese, Indian, and Indonesian migrants poured into Malaya as the tin and rubber industries expanded and the total population increased from 2,672,000 in 1911 to 5,511,000 in 1941.[23] Most of the newcomers produced tin and rubber in the west coast states south of Kedah and consumed rice. From 1920 to 1940 Malaya produced only about one third of its rice requirements.[24] The rice producers in Malaya were the Malays. In order to protect their traditional way of life which was oriented around the rice cycle the British administration enclosed the rice-producing lands in Malay reservations, the first of which was promulgated in the Federated Malay States in 1913. Non-Malays could not obtain grants or buy land in the reservations. A "Malay" was defined as a "person belonging to any Malayan race who habitually speaks the Malay language or any Malayan language and professes the Moslem religion".[25] This definition allowed immigrant Moslem Indonesians to own land in the reservations.

Race relations

The protectionist attitude of the British towards the Malay

farmer's traditional way of life was symptomatic of the Malayophilia which afflicted the Malayan Civil Service and affected policy in the Federated Malay States until the late 1930s. Chinese were not allowed to grow rice on a commercial scale; non-Malay labour thrown out of work during depressions in the tin and rubber industries was repatriated rather than being allowed to subsist on the land; and racial discrimination was practised in the granting of land for rice growing.[26] The Kerian scheme and the Sungai Manik irrigation scheme were therefore populated largely by "Malays" without patrimony.

The individualistic and sometimes scholarly early administrators were in touch with Malays of all classes and sometimes kept Malay mistresses. They gave way after Federation in 1896 to an elitist corp of bureaucrats dominated by public school-Oxbridge traditions and socially conscious *mems*. But in spite of the social chasm between the Malayan civil servant and his family and the Malay commoner, the image of the Malay as the "gentleman of the East" pervaded the Service. [27] The exclusiveness of the Malayan Civil Service, although owing something to British social traditions, was probably also an unforeseen by-product of the policy of indirect rule which in each state of the Federation encouraged the sultan and his circle to maintain the facade of Malay leadership and increase their status by a display of pomp and circumstance.[28] The service and the sultan were thus in status competition and the decentralization of the 1930s may be viewed as evidence of the latter's success in the struggle. The Unfederated Malay States were individually governed and Malays occupied offices at all levels of the administration. Throughout Malaya, the Malays, and immigrant Indonesians who identified with them, were in the position of most favoured son of the soil.

The Chinese on the other hand were regarded by the Malayan Civil Service as ungentlemanly mercenaries. They were encouraged before and just after Federation to expand their tin-mining enterprises in Perak and Selangor. But from the 1920s the proliferation of their economic activities was stopped wherever it threatened to undermine the economic security of Malay farmers, for example by the purchase of land.[29] The protectionist policy of the administration which cast the Malay in the role of rice grower may have been responsible for the decline of Malay entrepreneurship which was small-scale and dependent on individual initiative. The Chinese, on the other hand, were economically dynamic because they were marginal to the Anglo-Malay ruling cliques and had a high degree of social cohesion.[30] The Chinese in Malaya awoke to politics only after K'ang Yu-wei and Sun Yat-sen visited Malaya and Singapore, the latter repeatedly, in the period 1900-1910.[31] Even in the 1920s the majority of Chinese in Malaya were single men out to make money and return to China. There was no direct economic competition between Malays and Chinese in this period like that shown in the fights between rural bands of miners in the 1850s. The administration saw to it that Malays, Chinese, and Indians functioned in their allotted economic roles.[32]

The second world war

When the Japanese captured Malaya and Indonesia in 1941 they created a single administration for Malaya and Sumatra and thus once again spanned the Straits of Malacca. In the first phase of the occupation the Japanese attempted to use the prestige of the sultans to accustom the Malays to their role in the East Asia Co-prosperity Sphere. They also gave some support to Malayan youth organizations. As the war went against them they began to appease the Chinese and Indians and allow limited political power to the sultans. Precept and practice did not always coincide in their military administration. In spite of a policy of non-intervention in religious affairs they aroused opposition among Malays by their attempts at spiritual re-training in Japanese thoughtways. The reversion of the four northern states to Thailand and the presence in the jungle of the Malayan People's Anti-Japanese Army also probably contributed to the growth of a sense of unity which the Malays showed after the war.

Summary and conclusion

At the beginning of the nineteenth century the isolation of the Mandailingers in the land-locked Batak world in Sumatra was broken down and Mandailing society came under cultural and economic stress, a theme followed up in the next chapter. At the same time Malaya began to offer economic opportunities for

Sumatran miners and merchants, especially in the west coast states south of Kedah where most of the tin deposits were found. These opportunities diminished during the strife of the 1860s and 1870s and almost disappeared when, following political settlements, Chinese entrepreneurs dominated tin-mining. Towards the end of the nineteenth century however the introduction of new cash crops and a liberal land policy created fresh opportunities for Sumatran immigrants. The British protected the traditional "Malay" way of life but allowed economic exploitation of the countryside in the foothill zone to which many of the migrants had been attracted; the incoming groups were able to maintain their cultural identity, but many were forced to change to a new form of village economy based on cash crop production. The next chapter deals with the Mandailing response to the economic opportunities that they saw in West Malaysia and subsequent chapters with the cultural changes that followed when they accepted those opportunities.

The immigration and settlement of Mandailingers

Immigration before British intervention

The early Mandailing migrants to Malaya were probably adventurers whose temporary absence from their home village was in accordance with village custom. As single men they went out to seek their fortune; as men of the world they returned home, blessed or unblessed by fate, to marry and settle down. When Hindu states spanned the Straits, Central Sumatrans no doubt found their way to Malaya.[1] But this two-way flow of persons and goods was reduced as far as the Batak lands was concerned by the Islamization of Malaya under Malacca in the fifteenth century. The Mandailingers were culturally divided from the Malays until the early nineteenth century when they were converted to Islam during the Paderi wars (1810-30) in Sumatra. In the meantime, their Muslim neighbours, the Menangkabau, kept open the shortest line of communication across the Straits. During the Paderi wars and the following period of Islamic proselytization, the Mandailingers were provided with new motives for trade and travel. Conversion could entail a visit to Mecca or a religious centre in Malaya. The Menangkabau teachers who remained in Mandailing after the Paderis' military defeat initiated a Mandailing-Menangkabau rapprochement which could be continued in Malaya, and the Menangkabau who went to mine gold and tin in Malaya provided a model for the adventurous among the disbanded troops. No doubt after about 1820 a few Mandailingers visited Malaya.[2]

When hostilities ceased, the Dutch, who had fought with the Mandailingers against the Paderis, took over the administration and economic development of Mandailing. They set up collecting houses for local products and built a road to Natal on the southwest side of Sumatra in an effort to make the Mandailingers turn their backs on their trading partners on the Straits of Malacca. But this policy of economic containment could not work; the Mandailing area was economically upset by the war[3] and some parts of it had already reached their human carrying capacity.[4] A build up of migration to Malaya began and by the 1860s the Mandailingers were a recognizable social group there, with members engaged in mining, trading, mercenary activities, and economic and political mediation.[5]

We hear of them as feuding with the Bugis at To'Bandar Yasih's stockade at Kuala Lumpur and as occupying Raja Mahdi's fort on the hill at Kelang in 1866. In the same year "many of the leaders of the Mandilings at Kuala Lumpur retreated to Perak, though some remained in the stockade at Bukit Nanas". They were sufficiently consistent in their allegiance to draw the condemnation of Sultan Abdul Samad of Selangor who "reiterated to the world his trust in his son-in-law Tengku Kudin" saying "he has undertaken to vanquish the Mandilings and their allies. Now therefore the above (the local chiefs) will obey our son who is also appointed leader of all foreigners, and whosoever does not obey his orders will be treated as a rebel according to the law. All Chinese and Malays engaged in commerce in the interior shall assist Tengku Kudin with gunpowder and weapons. No Towkay shall assist the Mandiling people, and if by Allah's grace the disturbances are settled, the possessions of the Mandilings shall be divided among such of the aforesaid as assist Tengku Kudin."[6] In 1872 Said Mashor was again in the field with Mandailing and Rawa forces and cut off the Kuala Lumpur garrison. He was eventually defeated but what happened to the troops we do not know. We have heard already about Kulop Riau who "imported" a few hundred Mandailing to open mines at Sungai Raya about 1874.

The inferences we can draw from this scanty data are these. Mandailingers began to visit Malaya after about 1820 to work gold and tin in small groups which held together by virtue of their cultural distinction from other groups of miners such as Chinese and Bugis. There were enough of them by the 1860s for their social identity to be recognized by entrepreneurs and local political leaders. When displaced from their work in the tin belt of Perak and Selangor by local wars they banded together and found employment as mercenaries. The economic disruption of the Paderi war period stimulated their migration to Malaya; the economic disruption in western Malaya in the 1860s probably broke the pattern of migration. These Mandail-

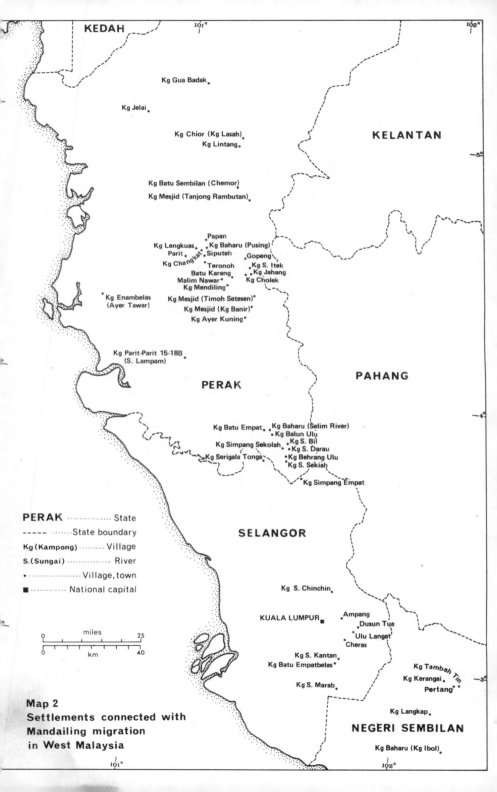

Map 2
Settlements connected with
Mandailing migration
in West Malaysia

ing migrants were adventurers or economic opportunists most of whom returned to their own country.

Mandailing immigration after 1874 (see map 2)

There is some evidence that Mandailingers were beginning to settle down in Malaya in the 1870s. There was apparently a "Korinchi (Mandiling)" (*sic*) village with six or seven ironworkers near Kuala Kampar and "Sungei Siput nearby was noted for its knives and spears";[7] there was a number of flourishing wet-rice growing villages on the Selim river below Changkat of which the population consisted of "foreign Malays, principally Mandelings" (Leech 1879); and Yap Ah Loy we are told "persuaded the Sumatran villages in Ulu Langat to plant padi".[8] The erstwhile tin miners and mercenaries were taking to the land and no doubt encouraged others from their homeland to join them.[9] Political and economic conditions in Sumatra did not entice Mandailingers in Malaya who had new opportunities to obtain land to return home and the irritations of Dutch rule caused the peasant population to consider settling elsewhere. The slaves were freed in 1870. In 1878 the culture system had its last fling when the Mandailingers in Sumatra were forced to plant coffee which was sold to the government at a fixed price. The scheme was soon abandoned, but it provided training in cash crop production which the Mandailingers were keen to put to use. Social and economic changes in Sumatra and favourable economic chances in Malaya started a new flow of migrants to Malaya towards the end of the century.

The new migrants sought the optimum conditions under which to practise their traditional economy and took part in cash crop production as smallholders when coffee and rubber were introduced. The pattern of migration of Mandailingers to Malaya from this early stage of the period of economic development under British influence until the present will now be explored using data from contemporary informants. I shall try to establish when present-day Mandailing communities were founded, where the early settlers came from, how they travelled to Malaya, and why they moved. I shall deal with leadership, local movement in Malaya, and the formation of communities with a mixture of Mandailing and other subcultural groups. The theme of the account is the search for freedom and economic stability.

Migrants on the move

The migration time scale

Two contemporary Mandailing communities were founded in the early 1870s when the period of feudalism and civil disturbance in Malaya was drawing to a close. If other Mandailing communities were founded in that era, their inhabitants have been absorbed into Malay society. Certainly there is no trace of them in social memory. The role of the Mandailingers as mercenaries must have led to their leaders being regarded as unpopular potential rivals by the local Malayan elite. Even under the British dispensation, no new Mandailing communities were founded for twenty years by such leaders. It was a religious teacher, not a potential political rival of the indigenous Malay rulers, who founded the next Mandailing community at Sungai Chinchin in 1892. (See figure 1.)

But at the turn of the century economic development and its opportunities dominated the minds of the Malayan administrators and the potential migrants. Twenty-four Mandailing communities were founded in western Malaya between 1899 and 1916. Most of them started in a small way at new sites, but five of them joined previously established settlements mostly at the fringe of the jungle. A few of the new communities were founded by people moving in search of the potentially best sites in western Malaya, but most of the founders came straight from Sumatra. And then the flow of founders ceased.[10]

From 1917 until the outbreak of World War II in Malaya only five new Mandailing communities were established, all as a result of internal movement within western Malaya. From the end of the war until 1968 four communities changed their site, all of them during the Emergency as a result of the Templer policy of bringing outlying communities under the control of the security forces. In summary, the immigration and settlement of Mandailingers in Malaya can be divided into six periods: the period of uncertainty from 1870 to 1891; the period of positive attraction from 1891 to 1950; the period of forced movement from 1951 to 1955; and the period of readjustment from 1956 to the present.

Mode of travel (see map 3)

All the founders (and all subsequent migrants) came from

Fig. 1.   Some Mandailing communities in West Malaysia by economic type

(The approximate date of founding is shown where known.*)

Economic Type			
Traditional Wet Rice	Non-traditional Wet Rice	Rubber-dominated	Pensions and Wages
Kg Baharu (Kg Ibol) 1951	Kg Balun Ulu 1912	Kg Baharu (Pusing) 1955	Kg Batu Empat-belas
Kg Batu Empat (Selim River) 1911	Kg S. Chinchin 1892	Kg Baharu (Selim River) 1955	Kg S. Kantan
Kg Kerangai 1926	Kg Chior (Kg Lasah) 1930	Kg Batu Sembilan (Chemor) 1905	Kg S. Marab
Kg S. Bil 1908	Dusun Tua 1912	Kg Cholek 1899	
Kg Tambah Tin 1955	Kg Gua Badak 1912	Kg Changkat 1873	
	Kg Jarong 1907	Kg Enambelas (Ayer Tawar) 1903	
	Kg Jelai 1905	Kerling 1904	
	Kg Lengkaus 1912	Kg Lintang 1910	
	Kg Parit-parit 15−18B (S. Lampam) 1939	Kg Mendiling 1910	
	Kg S. Sekia 1914	Kg Mesjid (Kg Banir) 1915	
	Kg Simpang Sekolah 1955	Kg Mesjid (Tanjong Rambutan) 1907	
	Ulu Langat 1916	Kg Mesjid (Timoh Setesen) 1916	
		Kg S. Itek 1901	
		Kg Serigala Tonga 1920	

*   Kg Simpang Empat and several places where there are very small Mandailing communities are not included.

inland villages in Sumatra. They had first to travel to the coast, make the sea journey to Malaya, and then go to their destination by road, path, or river transport. The length of the sea journey seems not to have been important. Once the decision to travel to Malaya had been made the migrants did not stop en route in Sumatra. Belawan (near Medan) was the favourite port of exit, a number preferred Sibolga, which shortened the land journey in Sumatra, and a few left from minor ports on the northwest coast of Sumatra like Tanjongbalai. The favourite port of entry was "Pulau Penang" (ap-

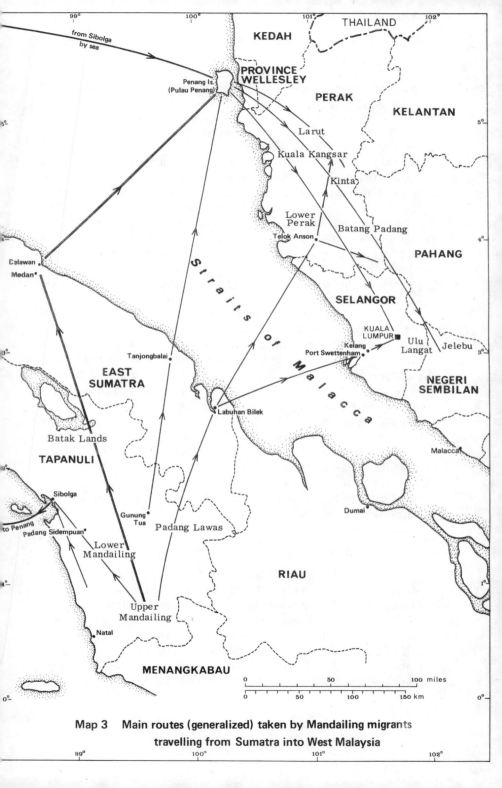

Map 3   Main routes (generalized) taken by Mandailing migrants
          travelling from Sumatra into West Malaysia

proximately 75 per cent). A few people came through Kelang and Telok Anson, but only the founder of Pusing, an itinerant merchant, entered, in 1873, by a port as far south as Malacca.

Why this preference for a northern port distant from many of the sites at which the Mandailing communities were founded? A shorter Straits crossing could be achieved by a landing at Kelang or Telok Anson. The answer is probably that "Pulau Penang" had become the established entry point for Mandailingers going to Kedah for religious training in the *pondok* (Islamic boarding) schools. A long sea journey was associated in the Mandailingers' minds with overseas travel, especially for religious purposes, since it was an integral part of the journey to Mecca. The majority of the Mandailing community founders moved about western Malaya for periods varying between two and twenty-three years before settling on a site; it is said explicitly of a few of them that they first went to Kedah for religious instruction. There are still a number of Mandailing individuals or small enclaves in Kedah whose immediate ancestors went to Kedah to attend a *pondok* school. It is likely therefore that in the period of uncertainty a number of Mandailingers visited Malaya via "Pulau Penang" for religious instruction; and that, while there, they assessed the possibilities of the country as a place for settlement. It is likely that the minority of Mandailing community founders who are said to have come straight from their village in Sumatra to the settlement site in Malaya had made a reconnaissance visit of this kind before finally leaving Sumatra. Belawan was a port of exit for the journey to Mecca, and "Pulau Penang", having become established as a port of entry for religious visits to Malaya, offered facilities which eased the entry of migrants into the country.[11]

Migrant leadership

Most of the village founders came from the fringes of the Mandailing region and not from the Mandailing heartland in Lower Mandailing. Of the communities that still exist in Malaya the first two to come into existence—at Pusing and Kg Changkat—were founded in the 1870s by men from Upper Mandailing. In the first half of the period of attraction the majority of founders were from Upper Mandailing. In the period of attraction as a whole nine community founders came from Upper Mandailing, four from Lower

Mandailing, three from Padang Lawas, and one each from Sipirok, Jambi, and Natal. On the available evidence we may conclude that the economically deprived Mandailing areas provided most of the migrants and that the migration movement started in Upper Mandailing.

The founders followed traditional patterns of behaviour for internal movement in Sumatra. First they indulged in the wander tradition of Mandailing young men. Young men according to this tradition leave their village for a period in order to seek their fortune in the outside world. If they are successful in establishing themselves as merchants or on the land they may send for or fetch their families. Although men who seek their fortunes in this way are sometimes helped by their relatives who have successfully emigrated, the tradition allows for the creation of new fortunes by pioneering. The emigrants are, in the Mandailing mind, temporary absentees. A clear distinction is drawn between temporary absence to seek a fortune (*merantau*) and removal of one's residence to some other place (*pindah*). When the latter occurs a ceremony symbolizing his removal from the control and help of the customary law (*adat*) of his natal village is held before the emigrant departs. Therefore when the emigrant arrives in a new area he must seek protection under the umbrella of a new customary law or create his own protective community. Seeking a fortune is the experimental phase of emigration, and may be repeated; it may or may not have a positive outcome such as removal of residence, or the emigrant's return with his fortune made. The second tradition followed by many of the founders concerns the way new settlements are created: in Sumatra they are normally created by a member of the elite (*raja*) family who leads a band of followers from a large settlement to a new site. When he does so he takes the customary law with him. The new settlement is tied, symbolically, politically, and by kinship, to the old. In this way mother-child village complexes are created.

Twelve of the thirty communities for which the relevant information is available were founded under *raja* auspices, four of them in the classic manner by *rajas* who emigrated from villages in Sumatra, and the rest under the control and protection of Sumatran *rajas* who managed to establish local control in Malaya; four were founded by religious leaders; two by men who were or subsequently became *hajis*; and two by merchants. The founders of two villages returned to Sumatra and left no relatives in the village so that their status is unknown; three villages were founded under the joint leadership of three or four men and five communities joined pre-existing villages founded by other sub-cultural groups (three Perak, one Tambuse, and one Pulau Penang Malay). It is evident that most Mandailing communities were founded by men whose traditional status promoted community cohesion, afforded some protection to members, and enhanced the general prestige of the community. The other communities protected themselves by acting as a group or by placing themselves under an existing local authority.

The members of the Mandailing elites who managed to establish local influence through political or economic means in Malaya played a very important role as cultural mediators for the Mandailing immigrants, but their sphere of authority was limited.

> Imam Perang Murungung, who is said to have taken part in the war against Pahang, was the first Mandailinger to settle in the Gopeng area. He died childless in 1914 and was buried at Gopeng. Informants say he was "D.O. (District Officer), *Penghulu*, Magistrate and anything else". Many Mandailingers came to Gopeng because Imam Perang was there. The water channels to the rice fields at Sungai Itek which Imam Perang made still exist. Sungai Itek was opened by Mandailingers under his direction. The *manggis* in front of the fish pond was planted by him. There were many Chinese here in his day. They liked him so much that at the breaking of the fast festival (a Muslim holiday) he was given many presents; he did not have to ask for anything. He had many buffaloes (a symbol of elite status in Sumatra) which he kept at Sungai Itek. At that time there was no fighting between sub-cultural groups because there was someone strong at the top, it is said. This situation is contrasted with the fighting which took place for three months in 1921 between Mandailing and Rawa men over a woman, when the police had to be called in. Imam Perang's younger half brother, Haji Abu Bakar, opened Kg Cholek in 1899 with the help of his mother's brother's son. He was "a man who helped the British and got a medal". A "cousin" of Imam Perang's, Haji Dollah, lived at Sungai Itek. He built a dam to bring water to Gopeng which was under the control of the Mandailingers. Osborne and Chapel (a British firm) used Haji Dollah as a labour recruiter. There was a hill near Sungai Itek called Gunung Haji Dollah. People used to come from Sumatra to work for two or three years, accumulate money and then return to Sumatra. He became so well known that people used to talk about going to work at Haji Dollah's.[12]

In Imam Perang's day Gopeng was run on a tender system for gambling and prostitution; the town was famous and Ipoh was unknown. But when larger-scale mining started in 1926 the administrative offices were rebuilt elsewhere and the town declined. There is now no Mandailing community there. Papan, the seat of a Mandailing *raja* line in central Perak, had a similar decline.

The *raja* line was started by Raja Asal who probably landed in Malaya in 1850-1860. He became headman of the Sumatra Malays in Kelang and was involved in the Selangor civil war. He died in the late 1870s. His son, known as Raja Belah, came to Papan on the entry of the British and became *Penghulu* there. He received a certificate of authority (*surat kuasa*) from the sultan. He announced that the customary law of Perak was to be followed, not that of Mandailing, but at weddings the speeches which symbolize the Mandailing social structure were made in the customary terms in the Mandailing language. The villages under him were Papan, Pusing, Teronoh, and Siputeh. He died in 1911 and was succeeded as *Penghulu* by his eldest son, who retired in 1937 and was succeeded by his younger brother. But the latter was replaced as *Penghulu* in 1940 by a non-family member under the new *Penghulu* system. There were no younger men in the family at the time.

A number of Mandailing communities were established in the area under Raja Belah. It was said everything stemmed from him; he was "father and mother to us all". A similar role was played in more recent times by the late Datok Agung of Behrang Ulu in Lower Perak.

Datok Agung's grandfather came from Sumatra; his father and he himself were born in Selayang, ten kilometres north of Kuala Lumpur. At the age of eight he was sent to a *pondok* school in Kedah for six years. He came to Behrang Ulu in 1916, gathered together some inhabitants of Batu 4 (Selim River) and established the village of which he became head. During the war he helped the British army and was afterwards decorated and made *Penghulu* of Behrang Ulu. He promoted the welfare of a number of Mandailing communities in the area and during the Emergency supervised the transfer of Kampong Jerni, then a completely Mandailing village, to Sungai Sekiah. Members of his family obtained good positions in the area and he eventually established a "town house" at Kg Baharu, a part of Selim River created during the Emergency, where there is also a Mandailing community. He died in 1967; the position of *Penghulu* has been filled by a career officer.

These examples demonstrate that a leader could function effectively as a father figure for the local Mandailing communities when he obtained a *Penghulu*ship. Formerly, from the point of view of the local population, the *Penghulu* was everything and the D.O. was not important. But statuses were changed in the nation-building phase. The pomp and circumstance which the British allowed the sultans at the state level was appropriate to their new political role, but it was not appropriate at the local level where authority derived from the indigenous political system was replaced by authority derived from the administrative bureaucracy.

Migrant motivation

Local irritations in Sumatra may have caused the Mandailingers to seek their fortune (*merantau*) in Malaya but the decision to migrate (*pindah*) was economically based. The pattern of visiting Malaya for religious education, as we have seen, was probably well established in the period of uncertainty, but towards the end of the nineteenth century economic pressures favouring *wanderungen* developed. The villages from which the early founders came were local administrative centres[13] or large villages in which there was the pressure on land resources. Factions there were (and still are) in these villages and there was traditional warrant for the hiving off of segments. By the end of the century, all the land in Upper Mandailing suitable for wet-rice growing by Mandailing techniques had been taken up, in fact the wet-rice areas on the map of 1904 are the same as those of today. Although coffee was introduced in the 1870s, this benefitted only the upland villages. There was no migration to Malaya from the large, coffee-growing villages of Upper Mandailing. In the low-lying villages on the other hand, the opportunities for cash crop production as an alternative to wet-rice production were limited. The migrants came from these villages. In contrast, the economic situation in Malaya encouraged migrants. Plantation rubber began in the 1890s; there was an improvement in land policy culminating in the compromise land code of 1897; and there was little pressure from Chinese workers who were still largely engaged in the tin industry. There was a peak in rubber prices in the 1910-12 period when the Malays turned rice land into rubber gardens and the liberal land policy made land readily available to Malays. No wonder that among the reasons given for the movement of those who founded villages in the period of attraction economic motives are found most often.[14]

Migration in the period of resettlement 1917-50

Changes in the Malayan economy and the comparative economic prospects of peasants in Malaya and Sumatra in this period affected the migration of Mandailingers. At the call of the village founders when they first arrived in Malaya came migrants many of whom worked for wages or supported themselves from quick-yielding cash crops like pineapples and bananas. They had scarcely had time to achieve economic security as the owners of wet-rice fields when they were surrounded by the changed economic circumstances of World War I. Rice shortages developed in Perak and many migrants in that state moved back to Sumatra where customary law gave them an indisputable right to a share of the yield of their ancestral rice fields in their village of origin. When this economic crisis passed, detailed information about the comparative economic advantages of Sumatra and Malaya was passed backwards and forwards by men who went to Malaya to try their luck or Mandailingers settled in Malaya who visited their village of origin in Sumatra in order to maintain social contacts.

The introduction of rubber into Upper Mandailing in 1918, from Malaya, according to local tradition, benefitted just those villages at a lower altitude from which the migrants had formerly come. In Malaya, on the other hand, the enclosure of the Malay Reservations, while protecting established communities, limited the horizons of prospective migrants and was symptomatic of the economic pressure which the Indians and Chinese were exerting on the Malay rural communities. A shortage of agricultural land was created in central Perak and especially in Kinta in the areas where a number of Mandailing settlements had been founded by the extension of large-scale tin mining. Pressure from the Chinese in the rural towns of Selangor and Perak forced the Malay traders out.[15] Thus new Mandailing communities were founded in the period of resettlement not by men fresh from Sumatra, but in response to population growth and local economic pressure. The Mandailing community, which had avoided cultural pressure from the surrounding matrilineally organized people by isolating itself in a mountain fastness at Langkap in the Kuala Pilah area of Negeri Sembilan, in 1926 outgrew its resources and established an off-shoot at Kerangai. A group of Mandailingers moved in 1930 five kilometres from Kg Lintang to Kg Lasah, originally founded by Perak people, allegedly in order to get better access to forest products; groups of displaced Mandailingers collected together in 1939 on a government irrigation project at S. Lampam, near Telok Anson; and isolated families or small groups moved out from their communities to take a place in the greater Malay polity at points of economic growth, e.g. Ulu Gali near Raub (Pahang), the furthest point of penetration of Mandailingers to the northeast. Some Mandailing communities at the same time declined or became extinct. At Kg Lengkuas for instance, which was founded near Parit in the heart of Perak by Kerinchi people in 1909 and expanded by an inflow of Mandailingers and Kampar men in 1912, some members of the Mandailing component went to Behrang Ulu, half went to Mecca, and some went back to Sumatra.[16] The Malays borrowed money from the *ceti* (Tamil moneylenders) but then could not pay the interest and were forced to sell their land to the *ceti* to pay off the debt. The *ceti* in turn sold the land to the Chinese. The Mandailing component of the very long-established village of Changkat in the same area which was under the patronage of Raja Belah of Papan suffered a gradual eclipse as its sponsor declined. The Kerinchi component of this village left about fifty years ago, the village was moved close to the road when the latter was made in the 1930s, and the Mandailingers identified themselves as members of the dominant Tolu group. Chinese shopkeepers in the nearby town of Pusing almost completely replaced the Malay merchants as rural production was replaced by mining, and the very long-established Mandailing community formerly also led by Raja Belah became socially invisible. The similar decline as a Malay centre of the market town of Gopeng in Kinta has been mentioned above (p. 27). In some of the nearby villages residents were disturbed by mining. There were formerly fifty to sixty Mandailing families in Kg Mendiling where there are now ten. The Mandailingers moved to Batu Karang and then to Mendok (about eleven kilometres from Malim Nawar), Jahang and Gopeng; and from Mendok back to Kg Mendiling, and to Kg Banir and Kg Lengkuas. There were formerly many Mandailingers at Batu Onam, between Tapah and Kampar, but they moved away when they sold their land for a tin mine. In short, during the period of resettlement, many of the Mandailing communities outside the Malay Reservations and not at the Malay pioneering fringe at the edge of the forest tended to lose their economic grip on their environment, and broke up. The communities which remained intact were differentiated by the addition of alien Mandailing and other Sumatran immigrant segments.

Movement during and after the Emergency

The enforced moves of the Emergency placed Mandailingers at Kg Baharu (Pusing) and Kg Baharu (Selim River) alongside people of sub-cultural groups such as Indian and Chinese whom they would not normally have admitted as neighbours. The almost purely Mandailing village of Kampong Jerni at Behrang Ulu moved to Simpang Sekolah, creating a multicultural village with an appendant village of Malayan Aborigines. The Mandailingers at S. Bil gained a group of Malayan Aborigines as neighbours, and the exclusively Mandailing village of Kerangai in Negeri Sembilan lost a segment which went first to Kuala Kelawang and then found an uncomfortable resting place on the outskirts of the Menangkabau town of Pertang.

After the Emergency, the Mandailingers resumed their normal practice of inter-village visiting and small economic units, usually single families, began a semi-nomadic search for economic success. Visits to Indonesia for a few months by older men with money started again, were broken off during the Confrontation period and then renewed with new vigour when Confrontation ended. Fortune seeking by younger men was along new lines: a search for success within Malaysia, either by entry into government service at levels which differed according to the degree of education they had been fortunate enough to get, or a move to the towns in search of a job in industry. There was, on the other hand, a growing group of persons of Mandailing origin retired from the public service living in high-class Mandailing enclaves like S. Kantan and S. Marab near Kajang.

Economic development and migration, 1800-1974: a summary

Migration to and within Malaya in the nineteenth and twentieth centuries was determined by land availability and the labour and finance required for economic production. In the early part of the nineteenth century there was a small flow of tin from the west coast states but the growth rate of the economy was small. Conditions for migrants were unstable. There were few Chinese in the country and the small bands of Sumatrans who came to seek their fortune in tin and gold mining returned home after two or three years. With the development of larger-scale tin mining by the Chinese after 1850, a large volume of Chinese labour was always moving in and out of the country. Under the unstable political conditions of the times tenure of agricultural land was very uncertain. This situation changed after British intervention. Moreover, in the period 1874-1900, with the further expansion of Chinese tin mining, the Indonesian immigrants were kept or pushed out of the tin industry onto the land where they could find a steadier living as agriculturalists. The entry of European enterprise in the tin industry forced the Chinese in turn into other economic activities in which they again threatened the Malays. The protectionist policy of the British, however, assured their land for the Malays but placed them in a limited set of roles as agriculturalists. They were rescued by the rise of rubber which gave them a significant place as producers of an important export. The situation was therefore favourable for Indonesian immigrants starting from scratch: they could easily acquire land; a cash crop which could be grown by one man was available to them; and they were treated by the administration as protected sons of the land.

The policy of easy land acquisition for Malays was continued after World War II. There was a population movement (during the Emergency) towards existing settlements around which the land was more intensively utilized, and a movement during and after the Emergency, owing to population pressure or the encroachment of mines on agricultural land, from existing villages to government set-tlement schemes. The unstable conditions of the Emergency period kept Indonesian migrants away and during Confrontation travel from and to Indonesia was not possible. There was therefore no ad-dition to the pool of Mandailing immigrants in Malaya who were subjected to almost twenty years of Malayanization without contact with the culture of their area of origin.

In summary, the majority of the pre-1890 Mandailing migrants either returned to Sumatra or were absorbed into the Malay polity, but from 1891 to 1916 Malaya had positive economic advantages for Sumatran immigrants and groups which still survive were formed under traditional leaders. In the period 1917-50, however, the com-parative economic advantage of Malaya over Sumatra from the migrant viewpoint disappeared and economic pressures inside Malaya forced a redistribution of settlement. The enforced moves of the Emergency period and the post-Emergency search for new avenues to economic success led to further population movements. Overall, there has been a decrease in cultural isolation and a breakdown of geographical isolation.* Some Mandailingers have been incorporated into culturally alien communities and some culturally alien segments have been incorporated into Mandailing communities. Multicultural units have been formed whose elements are in a relationship of symbiotic convenience. The result is a variety of sociological settings in which elements of Mandailing culture display varying degrees of survival.

These varied social groups constitute the Mandailing presence in Malaya: the culturally isolated communities of Negeri Sembilan; the schools, villages, and small groups in Selangor and Kedah; the kinship-connected and culturally heterogenous villages of central Perak; the socially invisible Mandailing segments in market towns; and the enclaves of relatively wealthy retired men and widows. They are a consequence of the Mandailing search for security and economic success. I shall now describe the political and economic context and the size and structure of these contemporary Mandailing groups.

Cultural change in Mandailing communities: economy and language

This chapter begins with an account of Mandailing culture as it was in Sumatra from 1892 to 1917. In this period, all but two of the founders of present-day Mandailing communities in Malaya left their homeland. In this span of twenty-five years there was little cultural change in any one part of the Mandailing area because Islamization had been completed, the period of forced cultivation of coffee had ended, the system of administration had reached a stable state, and rubber had not yet been introduced. In other words the founders who came at the beginning of this period and those who came at the end brought the same culture with them. But can it be assumed that all founders came from one culture area when some came from Upper Mandailing which is mountainous and some from Lower Mandailing, which had large areas of flat land? Although these areas were different ecologically they were not very different culturally: in the flatter areas there was a concentration on wet-rice growing; and in the mountains a diversity of crops including coffee, cinnamon, and cloves as cash crops and wet rice and dry rice as subsistent crops. This difference can safely be ignored by making the assumption that some crops of all types were grown in all districts and that the techniques of production were everywhere much the same.[1]

The subsistence crop was everywhere wet rice, supplemented where necessary by dry rice and sweet potato, *ubi*, grown on hillside fields whose location was changed every two or three years, *ladang*.[2] The division of labour for the latter was quite simple: the men did the heavy clearing work, the women did the lighter clearing work, planted the crop, and cared for it while it was growing. For wet-rice production, there was a more complicated division of labour: the men looked after the dams and waterways; the women tilled the fields, and sowed the seed-beds; the men and youths planted out the seedlings; the women weeded the growing crop; the men harvested the crop; the women did the winnowing; and the men repaired the rice barn and carried home the bulk of the crop. Men and women were responsible for magic on the rice fields.

Extended households were important economic units each comprised of a group of male agnates who inherited and owned the wet-rice fields in common and worked them together. These groups were the smallest units in a patrilineally organized society in which the key units were lineages of different span, *kahangi*, and clans, *marga*. Patrilineal and affinal kinship ties linked together people from a fairly wide area. In each village there were members of three or four clans and one of these, the dominant clan, provided the *raja*, or ruler.

Fig. 2.   Kinship terms for aunts, uncles, and some cousins (Mandailing, Sumatra)

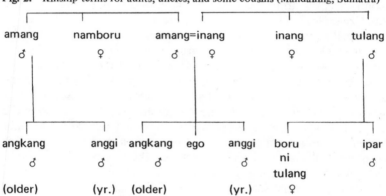

The group from which a man took his wife he called his *mora*, wife-giving group, and he honoured that group. He in turn was honoured by his *anak boru*, i.e. the group to a member of which a woman of his group was given in marriage. This asymmetry was preserved by the preference for a man to marry his real or classificatory mother's brother's daughter and this preference was expressed by using a special kinship term for that relative so that she was distinguished from other cousins.[3]

The kinship terminology for aunts, uncles, and cousins (shown in figure 2) reflected the dominance of the patrilineal principle and also the principle that the social relationships among clans were asymmetrical.

A marriage could be effected in various ways. In a proposal marriage, *manjapaek*, a formal request for the hand of a girl was made to the girl's relatives by representatives from the prospective groom's party; in an abduction marriage, the girl was taken from her house by the prospective husband and his kinsmen and taken to their house.[4] In whatever way the marriage was effected, the union was socially sanctified by a series of customary law wedding ceremonies which included lengthy speeches from all parties concerned. After the wedding, the couple lived in the groom's father's house for about two years. The marriage entailed two payments: the Little Gold, a payment made in cash or kind by the groom's party to the close relatives of the bride and supposed to be used to buy her finery; and the Great Gold, a large payment whose quantity was determined by the social status of the bride. This payment supposedly was made by the groom's group to the bride's group, but in fact was never paid.[5] In customary law, the Great Gold symbolized the debt owed by a wife-receiving group to its wife-giving group. The stability of the social system depended upon two key elements: the ownership of wet-rice fields in common by a group of agnates, which assured the continuity of the patrilineage organization and related the kinship system to the system for economic production; and the concept of asymmetrical alliance which determined the relative status of different patrilineal kinship groups and their ties in marriage.

A man's initial social position was determined by kinship, but he could improve his economic standing by entrepreneurial activity as a carpenter, ironsmith, sugar-maker, herdsman, gatherer of forest products, or trader. He could increase his influence in the village community by becoming a medicine man or religious teacher, but unless he was born into the right lineage, he could not gain any political power. The Dutch policy of indirect rule and economic control assured opportunities for significant advancement only for the established *raja* families. The men who founded the Mandailing communities in Malaya, judging from their activities, were attempting to escape from this social straightjacket. They were prepared to accept cultural change and adjustments in social relations which aided their economic advancement and legitimized their new role as leaders.

Established village economies

Most Mandailing villages in Malaysia have one of two kinds of economy, i.e. subsistence base plus cash crop, or cash crop alone. The normal subsistence crop is wet rice. Dry rice is the sole form of rice production in only one village and occurs in combination with wet rice in two others. Rubber is produced as a cash crop in all Mandailing communities except one. The exception is Parit-parit 15-18B, S. Lampam, which forms part of the S. Manik irrigated rice scheme. Fruits are important as a fairly regular source of income in two villages in combination with rubber. There are therefore two major types of economy: wet rice plus rubber and rubber plus ancillary economic activities such as dry-rice growing, fruit growing, and wage earning. There are a few communities consisting almost entirely of pensioners. (See figure 1.)

The entailments of wet-rice production are: a set of operations which must be carried out in sequence beginning at a certain season; a high yield once a year followed by an off season with no yield; concentration of manual labour at peak periods; and high rentals for those who do not own their own wet-rice fields. The main physical requirement for wet rice is permanent fields with an ample supply of water. Dry-rice production entails a fixed cycle of operations, heavy work at a certain point in the cycle, and dependence on weather for a good yield. The main physical requirement is an extensive area of land for which other uses are not in competition. When a rubber garden is established, dry rice can be grown in the garden for the first year or so, but there is then a period of four or five years before the rubber trees are tappable. A regular weekly yield up to a certain limit can be got from an established garden with light labour. The tenure requirements are the use of a minimum of nearly a hectare for fifteen years (some smallholders' gardens are up to thirty years old but they yield poorly and are uneconomic to work under present conditions). Fruit trees are grown round the house or in small plots of up to nearly a hectare. The yield is seasonal and uncertain. In short, rice production lends itself to a complicated division of labour and breaks up the year into sections each characterized by a certain type of work; rubber production calls for little skill and offers a cash return on the same day for labour expended; and fruit production requires little labour but cannot be relied upon as a source of income.

Nine of the fourteen villages that are dominated by rubber growing without wet rice are concentrated in the Kinta District and the northern part of the Batang Padang District in a foothill zone where large-scale tin mining has been carried on since 1911. The enormous holes made by the mines, some of them several hundred metres across and sixty metres deep, have eaten into the area available for agriculture and disturbed the natural drainage. The physical conditions necessary for wet-rice growing have gradually disappeared. The villages in this area have a history of breakup and movement and in several villages former rice fields have been abandoned. One of the rubber-dominated villages, Kg Enambelas (Ayer Tawar), is in the Dindings District in a position where water is hard to control and three others are near market towns (Kajang, Kerling, and Selim River) in the foothill zone in southern Perak and central Selangor. In short, the rubber-dominated villages are in situations where the physical conditions for wet-rice growing have been progressively eroded and are not now fulfilled.

Fourteen of the seventeen villages in which wet rice is combined with rubber are in the foothill zone of Perak and Selangor to the north and south of the area in which large-scale tin mining has been carried on and three are in the mountain zone of Negeri Sembilan. The physical situation of these villages is therefore similar to the pre-tin mining ecology of the majority of the rubber-dominated villages and in a number of the latter wet rice was formerly grown. The difference between the two styles of village economy is therefore due to differences in extrinsic economic factors expressed as differences in land utilization.

Fig. 3. Ownership of wet-rice fields, percentage of Mandailing families in the village and number of Mandailing families

Type of Economy	% of Families Owning Wet-Rice Fields	% of Mandailing Families of Total in the Village	Mean Number of Mandailing Families	Number of Villages
Wet-rice	65 or more	86–100	25.4	5
Wet-rice	5–48	25–74	24.3	9
Rubber	0	15–79	17.0	12
Pensions and wages	0	?	13.3	3

The contrast is sharpened by differences in development plans. In the Kinta District the area available for land development is very small indeed. There are two controlled alienation schemes and a small number of fringe alienation schemes. Tin mining takes precedence over all other types of land use. Some areas have been reworked a number of times as tin prices have risen and new techniques have been developed. There is no security of tenure and therefore a reluctance to invest in land re-development for agriculture. Development is concentrated on minor works such as children's playgrounds, *sepak raga* grounds,[6] meeting halls, village pathways, bridges, and water channels. In contrast, most of the wet-rice growing villages are in areas where there are extensive land development schemes.[7] These schemes are not carried out at the expense of minor works. In Jelai, which is a Local Council area, for example, construction has included a prayer house costing M$10,000, and a concrete drain costing M$2,000. The Mandailing wet-rice growing communities in Negeri Sembilan are less well served. Two of them had to move during the Emergency and are forced to hire wet-rice fields from the local Malays. They have reserve wet-rice land, however, in their original village to which a number of people are now returning. The contrast that has become increasingly clear over the past fifty years is that in wet-rice growing villages there are economic opportunites while in rubber-dominated villages there are not.

This economic situation is reflected in the size and composition of the villages. The mean number of households is larger in villages in which wet rice is grown. Among wet-rice growing villages a clear distinction can be drawn between those villages in which more than 65 per cent of household heads own wet-rice fields and those in which less than 50 per cent own wet-rice fields. In the former, the total population is smaller but more than 86 per cent of the households in each village are Mandailing. On the other hand, in the villages with fewer wet-rice owning families, the mean percentage of Mandailinger families is only 50 per cent.[8] In rubber-dominated villages Mandailingers comprise 54.3 per cent of the population on the average. In the villages with much wet-rice ownership and a very large Mandailing component the mean number of Mandailing families is 25.4; in the other wet-rice growing villages it is 24.3; in rubber-dominated villages it is 17; and in communities which rely on pensions and wages it is 13.3 (see figure 3). The smaller size of the

Mandailing component in the rubber-dominated villages as compared with the wet-rice growing villages probably reflects the breakup of villages caused by mining. On the other hand in the now rubber-dominated villages the Mandailing component is slightly larger relative to the rest of the population. This suggests that the rubber-dominated villages are segments of larger villages with a substantial Mandailing majority that formerly existed in the same area if not at the same site and that in the face of economic pressure tending to fragment the village the Mandailing components maintain their integrity.

There are Banjarese in eight of the twenty-nine villages in which the Mandailing component accounts for more than 5 per cent of the population but they never account for more than 5.8 per cent of the total population (this figure is reached only in one village). There are Javanese in fourteen villages. They comprise more than 5 per cent of the village population only in Kg Enambelas, where the proportion in the population has been swollen by Javanese who were released after a period of indenture on a nearby Dutch-owned rubber plantation. The other two major groups found in villages in which there are Mandailingers are indigenous Malays (including internal migrants from Petani, Pulau Penang, and other Malay states) and other Sumatrans.[9] Representatives of both these groups are found in sixteen villages and representatives of one or the other in eight more.[10] Mandailingers, and other Sumatrans, live in the same village as Chinese or Indians only in a small number of New Villages formed during the Emergency. (See map 4.)

The relationship between village size and composition and economic context can be summarized in the following typology. There are five villages of small to moderate size with a large Mandailing component and in which 65 per cent or more of the members own wet-rice fields; nine villages of moderate to large size in which the Mandailing component varies from 25 per cent to 74 per cent and 5 per cent to 48 per cent of the population own wet-rice fields; twelve rubber-dominated villages of medium size in which the Mandailingers comprise 15 per cent to 79 percent of the population; and three small communites of Mandailingers who are either pensioners or wage earners (see figure 3). There are also a number of villages in which the Mandailing component numbers less than five families comprising less than 5 per cent of the population.

The highly monetized economy of the rubber-dominated vil-

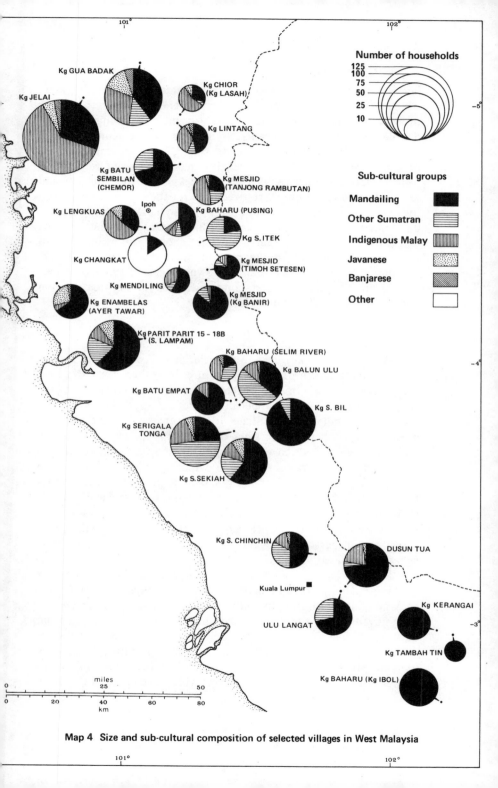

Map 4 Size and sub-cultural composition of selected villages in West Malaysia

lages contrasts with the subsistence orientation of the villages in which wet rice is grown. In the latter farmers have a larger number of side-lines and attempt to be self-sufficient by growing coconuts, double-cropping, growing maize by *gotong royong* (communal effort), using different methods of pounding rice, and making fishponds. Cooperatives for purposes like making loans of capital and timber getting, which require the same kind of coordination and recognition of common interest required for the control of water on the wet-rice fields, are commoner in these villages. The rubber-dominated villages on the other hand have a larger number of wage earners and a slightly larger number of shops. The availability of cash is reflected also in the pattern of expenditure: in rubber-dominated villages 1 in 17.9 families owns a car and 1 in 9.4 families owns a motor cycle; the corresponding figures for wet-rice growing villages are 1 in 27 and 1 in 12.3.[11]

Agriculture

Wet rice is the key crop in the relations between the economic and social systems in Mandailing culture, but other crops, dry rice, edible root crops *ubi*, maize, vegetables, and fruits, form part of the subsistence complex. In rubber-dominated villages, dry rice is not now grown,[12] but in three villages it is remembered as a catch crop grown in the rubber gardens when they were first planted. In wet-rice growing villages, dry rice was grown during the 1960s in two villages as a catch crop before rubber and in two other villages irregularly in separate fields. In these four villages, over 60 per cent of the population is Mandailing. The percentage of persons owning wet-rice fields varies from 12 to 65. In short, dry rice is still grown as a catch or irregular crop in some 30 per cent of wet-rice growing villages in which not all persons own wet-rice fields but is not now grown in rubber-dominated villages.

Root crops *ubi* are grown as a separate crop in four wet-rice growing villages. Three of these are villages with a high percentage of Mandailingers in the population, the fourth village is one which was moved during the Emergency and has become separated from its wet-rice fields. In one rubber-dominated village, root crops are spoken of as crops for bad times and in two others a little is regularly planted. Maize is grown as a separate crop by *gotong royong*, communal effort, in one wet-rice growing village, and in another as a catch crop on the wet-rice fields. Both these villages have a high percentage of Mandailingers in the population and 48 per cent to 65 per cent of the population own wet-rice fields. Maize is not grown in rubber-dominated villages. All villagers like to have an area of land (up to nearly a hectare) on which to grow fruit trees and a variety of vegetables, *dusun* or *kampong*. This generalization is true of the Mandailing community on the government-sponsored wet-rice scheme at Sungai Lampam where there is a surplus of wet-rice, and of the rubber-dominated villages.

In summary, in wet-rice villages with a dominant Mandailing population, the agricultural subsistence complex, in so far as it is represented in the growing of catch and supplementary crops, maintains the form it had in the Mandailing culture of Sumatra, even in villages in which about half or less of the population own wet-rice fields; while in rubber-dominated villages, the subsistence crop complex occurs in attenuated form as orchards and vegetable gardens. In the latter it is clear that rubber replaces rice, the main "subsistence" crop, and other supplementary staples such as maize and root crops are not usually grown.

After the Islamization of Mandailing in the nineteenth century, one of the most remarkable phenomena of cultural integration was the adjustment in Mandailing of the rice cycle to the Islamic lunar calendar. The latter is eleven days shorter than the solar calendar so that when agriculture became tied to it there was a precession of the agricultural cycle with respect to the seasons. This arrangement could be strictly adhered to only where there was no marked dry season. But on the west side of West Malaysia, there is a marked difference in wet and dry periods owing to monsoon influences, hence the process of Islamization of the agricultural cycle had to be reversed. The start of the wet-rice cycle is now associated with the Islamic calendar in only three villages and with the solar calendar in the remainder. Most of the latter rely on the announcements made in each district by the Agricultural Service about the correct date on which to start each phase of the rice cycle. These dates are enforced only on the government-sponsored development projects (such as S. Manik); in other places the village communities demonstrate some independence by holding a meeting of owners or an inter-village meeting to determine the date on which the rice cycle shall start. Advice is taken from the government, but the aim of the villagers is to avoid heavy work in the fasting month.

Fig. 4. Participation in phases of the wet-rice production cycle in Mandailing communities in Malaysia and Sumatra

M = men; B = both men and women take part; W = women. Figures are the number of villages in which the practice is carried out as shown. Traditional practice in Sumatra is in italic.

Hoeing	Building Walls	Sow-ing	Plant-ing Out	Weed-ing	Guard-ing	Reaping	Thresh-ing	Winn-owing	Winnow-ing by Hand
M2	M	M2	*M3*	M	M	*M5*	M5	M	M
B6	B5	B5	B5	B4	B1	B2	*B3*	B2	B
W	*W2*	*W*	W1	*W3*	*W2*	W1	W2	*W4*	*W3*

If wet rice is a key element in Mandailing culture, the survival of the traditions associated with its cultivation should be an indicator of the survival of Mandailing culture as a whole. Of the production sequence outlined above (p. 34), those activities most strongly supported by traditional magico-religious beliefs and definitive of the division of labour were sowing, planting out and reaping. The first was carried out by women, the last two by men. Among the Mandailingers in Malaysia, sowing is no longer carried out only by women in any village from which a report was obtained,[13] and in over half the villages men have lost their prerogative of planting out. On the other hand, reaping and winnowing are carried out in Malaysia in much the same way as they were in Sumatra. In general there has been a move towards participation by both husband and wife in every phase of wet-rice production (see figure 4 and plates 1 and 2).[14]

The only villages in which the division of labour in the wet-rice cycle approximates to the traditional Mandailing practice is one of the five villages in which there is an overwhelming proportion of Mandailingers in the population and in which more than 65 per cent of the people own wet-rice fields. In all other villages, traditional practices on the wet-rice fields, like language, demonstrate a phenomenon of cultural replacement associated with the introduction of rubber. Tasks formerly carried out by one sex or the other are now carried out by both working together perhaps with a division of labour within the task. For example reaping, which was formerly carried out by men only, is carried out in two phases: in the first, men reap with the reaping hook *sabit*; and in the second, women cut

Plate 1.   Village life: wooden walled houses with iron or thatched roofs, well-swept paths and shady palms

Plate 2.   Village life: preparing the wet-rice fields by hand

with the cutting knife *tuwai*. The preparation of the rice fields has been affected by recent technological change. In Sumatra the fields in Mandailing are hoed, mostly by women; up to 1965 in most Mandailing communities in Malaya the hoeing was done by men and women working together, but since 1965 small mechanical cultivators have been introduced and these are operated solely by men.[15]

Four types of villages have been distinguished: wet-rice villages in which a large number of households own wet-rice fields; villages with a mixed wet-rice and rubber economy; villages which are economically dependent on rubber alone; and villages in which the main sources of income are pensions and wages. Each type of village has been shown to have definite demographic and cultural features. It has been suggested that some former wet-rice growing villages have evolved into rubber-dominated villages owing to regional ecological changes. It is in these villages that Mandailing culture has changed the most. As long as wet-rice growing continues the cultural complex and subsistence orientation associated with it persists, but once this pattern breaks down it is very difficult to reinstate it and usually it is ecologically impossible to do so because the conditions required for growing wet rice no longer exist and, moreover, it is not possible to grow substitute subsistence crops because of a shortage of land.

Some cultural changes take place in villages as a response to general social and climatic conditions in Malaya, e.g. the change from a lunar to a solar agricultural calendar and changes in division of labour, but some changes take place only in villages of a specific economic type. We shall now explore the relationship between language, the cultural phenomenon par excellence, village economic type, and the size of the Mandailing community.

The persistence of the Mandailing language

Language puts a cultural mark upon a man. In England, speech reveals social identity;[16] in the Malay world, the form of speech used varies according to the relative status of speaker and spoken to. Each of the immigrant sub-cultural groups in West Malaysia had its own language: Achinese, Batak, Menangkabau, Javanese, Banjarese, Chinese, and Tamil.[17] In common with other immigrants, the Mandailing adventurers who left their homeland to seek their fortune learnt Malay, the lingua franca of the Malacca Straits area. They used Malay in contacts with the administration and other sub-cultural groups, and Mandailing within their own communities. But as these communities came into closer contact with other sub-cultural groups, their children spoke Malay (or some other local "lingua franca" like Javanese) more frequently than they spoke Mandailing. The latter became the language of the elders. This change in the function of Mandailing has reached various stages in contemporary Mandailing communities.

The Mandailing language is used more in wet-rice growing villages than in rubber-dominated villages; all the villages in which the language is used in everyday speech are wet-rice growing villages. I shall refer to those villages in which the language is spoken by most or some residents as high usage villages and the other villages as low usage villages. Ten out of thirteen wet-rice villages are high usage villages whereas only two out of eleven rubber-dominated villages are in the same category. This can be explained perhaps by the high importance attached to wet-rice growing in Mandailing culture. Wet-rice growing determines the yearly round of agricultural activities, specifies many of the economic roles of men and women, is the key to lineage organization and contributes largely to the Mandailing vocabulary. Rubber, on the other hand, has only relatively recently become part of the Mandailing economic repertoire and was unknown to the founders of the Mandailing communities before they left Sumatra. For the Mandailingers in Malaya, the language of rubber cultivation is Malay.

Absolute size of the Mandailing community is also associated with language usage: communities of twenty or more families have high language usage; communities with five to twenty families have low. But the effect of absolute size is greater in wet-rice growing villages than it is in rubber-dominated villages. There are three large (more than twenty family) rubber-dominated Mandailing communities with low language usage, whereas large wet-rice growing villages are almost certain to have high language usage. The association of high language use with high percentage of Mandailingers in the village population is greater than it is with absolute size of the Mandailing community. In ten of the fifteen villages in which the Mandailingers comprise 50 or more per cent of the population, there is high language usage, whereas in the nine villages in which they comprise less than 50 per cent of the population language use is high in only two communities. But again rubber exerts an effect: there is no significant difference in language usage between those rubber-dominated villages which have 50 per cent or more Mandailingers and those which have less than 50 per cent. There are few wet-rice villages with less than 50 per cent Mandailing component, but the indications are that when Mandailingers are in a minority language use becomes depressed. In short, wet-rice sustains the use of the Mandailing language, even though only a small percentage of the population own wet-rice fields. The limiting point is reached when the Mandailing community becomes a minority (say 25 per cent) of the total village population. At this point, the self-sustaining effect of the cultural constellation associated with wet-rice growing gives way to the need for cultural accommodation with the dominant majority. In villages which become dependent on rubber alone, the language loses its function as a living tool, no matter what the absolute or relative size of the Mandailing component.

Cultural change in Mandailing communities : social organization

In this chapter relationships between village economic type and kinship terminology, social groups, marriage patterns, frequency of divorce, types of inheritance, and magico-religious organization are explored. Cultural features that are found to be significant are used to create a new typology of village and the analysis concludes with an account of the way various features are clustered.

Kinship

There is a sequence of changes in kinship terminology under conditions of cultural contact which we shall assume can be reconstructed by comparing the terminologies used in contemporary communities. We shall first try to establish the sequence, second, look for changes in the sequence which indicate critical changes in the social system, and third, relate these changes to other differences in Mandailing communities.

The asymmetrical marriage system and the preference for marriage with a real or classificatory mother's brother's daughter which are features of traditional Mandailing culture in Sumatra are reflected in the kinship terminology.[1] A man calls his father's sister, who will be given in marriage to a group which is wife-receiving to his own, by a special term; he calls his mother's sister, who will be given in marriage to a member of his own group, by a special term; his mother's brother, who is his prospective father-in-law, he calls by the same term as wife's father; his mother's brother's son, i.e. the brother of his prospective wife, he calls by the same term as wife's brother; and by similar reasoning, calls his father's sister's son by the same term as he calls his sister's husband. All grandparents are called by the same term. (See figure 1.)

Fig. 5. Kinship terminologies in use among Mandailingers in Malaya

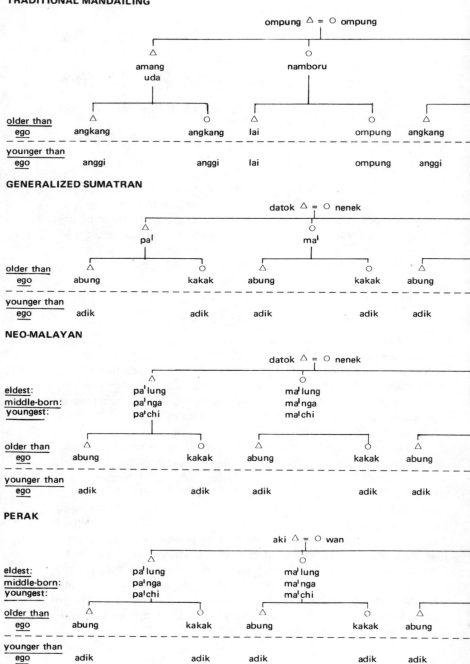

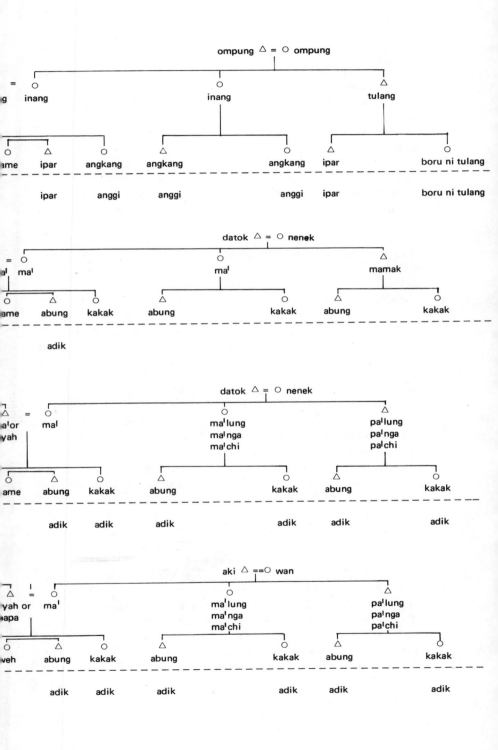

This traditional Mandailing terminology survives intact or nearly intact in five villages.[2] The first change that takes place is the loss of the special term for father's sister, who is then called by the same term as mother, and the second is the loss of special terms for mother's brother's son and father's sister's son who are called by the terms used for brother. (See figure 5.)

The next important change is the dropping of the Mandailing term for mother's brother and the substitution of the Menangkabau term *mamak*; at the same time all other terms which differentiate among other parents' siblings are dropped and all cousins are called by Malay terms used for siblings. The latter differentiate between persons older and younger than the speaker, and among those older than the speaker between males and females. The Mandailing term for sister's husband is dropped and the term for wife's brother is used as a self-reciprocal term. Special terms are used for male and female grandparents; for father's father, the Mandailing term is replaced by the Menangkabau term *datok*. Father-in-law and mother-in-law are called *pa'mentua* and *ma'mentua* respectively and a child-in-law is called *manantu*. These last three terms are used in Negeri Sembilan (Swift 1965, p.176). These changes produce a terminology which I shall call Generalized Sumatran which is found in ten villages, in one of which it occurs alongside Traditional Mandailing.

The special term for mother's brother, *mamak*, is then dropped so that there is now no difference in the terms applied to different categories of parents' siblings. But the occupants of any category are distinguished by using secondary terms which indicate birth order. For example, a father's sister is called *ma'lung, ma'nga,* and *ma'chi* according to whether she is the eldest, middle-born, or youngest female in her sibling group respectively. The self-reciprocal term *ipar* for wife's siblings is still used. This type of terminology I shall call Neo-Malayan. It is found in six villages.

A type of terminology which I shall call Perak[3] also occurs in which extensive use is made of the terms which differentiate according to birth order, the *ipar* terminology used for wife's siblings is dropped, and grandparents are called by a non-Menangkabau term. This terminology occurs in two Mandailing communities, but in one of these it has been almost completely displaced by Personalized Malay in which birth order terms are dropped and an individual is distinguished by the appropriate term followed by his name.

The first change in social arrangements indicated in this series of terminologies is the dropping of the asymmetrical relations between large social groups which has probably occurred in some villages using Traditional Mandailing terminology. The last trace of a Mandailing style asymmetry disappears in Generalized Sumatran with the introduction of self-reciprocal term for sister's husband. Structurally we are left with a terminology which could lend itself to the patrilineal emphasis of Mandailing culture or the matrilineal emphasis of Menangkabau culture. There is evidence of Menangkabau influence other than the use of the Menangkabau term for the key role of mother's brother: the occasional use of *biras* for wife's sister's husband; and the use of Menangkabau terms for wife's father, wife's mother, son's son, and father's father.

In Neo-Malayan, the last traces of asymmetry disappear. We have a terminology indicative of a bilateral kinship system in which equal emphasis is placed on descent through both men and women, and the kindred rather than the lineage is the important social grouping. The Perak terminology emphasizes primogeniture. It is the kind of terminology which could be taken up by a group trying to identify with the indigenous Malay social system in which a good deal of emphasis is placed on titles, rank, and status. The use of names instead of kinship terms in Personalized Malay is probably a result of Western influence. Names are sometimes used among young people even in communities which use a Generalized Sumatran terminology.

Terminology

It is not suggested that the above series represents a necessary sequence through which all communities must pass. Traditional Mandailing is clearly the terminology with which every Mandailing community started, but theoretically any other system could replace it, Westernization could occur rapidly for example in whole or in part at any stage, but the facts are that the alternative terminologies occur together in such a way as to form an overlapping series. Moreover, villagers frequently know terms which have fallen out of use and these known but unused terms are always from a terminology earlier in the sequence. In some villages the old and the young speak different languages and the process of change is evident in the use of different terms for the same kinship position.

There is a strong association between Traditional Mandailing terminology and the five villages in which the Mandailingers comprise 86 per cent or more of the population and in which 65 per cent or more of the people own wet-rice fields. Four of the five Traditional Mandailing users are in this category.[4]

There is a fairly strong association between type of kinship terminology and use of the Mandailing language. In villages in which language use is high, Traditional Mandailing and Generalized Sumatran are found; where language use is low, Neo-Malayan takes over. But terminology is more conservative than language and Generalized Sumatran sometimes hangs on when language use is low. In general, however, terminology shows the same kind of association as language; Generalized Sumatran is commoner in the larger non-traditional, wet-rice using villages, Neo-Malayan in the smaller villages dominated by rubber.

In sum, although types of kin terminology depend on village history there is a general sequence of changes through which kinship terminology seems to pass. We shall explore the parallels between this sequence and changes in the social units of which Mandailing communities are composed in the next section.

Social groups

Traditional Mandailing social organization in Sumatra had four key concepts: *marga* = patriclan; *kahangi* = lineage; *mora* = wife-giving group; and *anak boru* = wife-receiving group. Every person knew his clan identity and that he could not marry within the clan. The lineage was the group with whom a man acted in concert in everyday affairs and to whom he looked for support in matters of customary law; his wife-giving group was the patrilineage to which a man gave honour and service; and his wife-receiving group the patrilineage from which he received honour and service.

In Malaysia these concepts have been re-defined, replaced, and used in non-traditional ways. *Marga* is usually defined as referring to origins, or more specifically as origin traced through father. Sometimes it simply means *saudara*, brothers in a general sense. The notion of unilineal descent survives in the Menangkabau word *suku*, most frequently substituted for *marga*, which means matriclan in Menangkabau, and Negeri Sembilan. Other words substituted for

marga are *bangsa*, race and *puak*, party or group. The Mandailingers in Malaysia think that one's *marga* provides a means of
indentification in strange places; it has *adat* (customary law) use in
Sumatra they say. Every older man knows his own *marga*, and keeps
it as a private stand-by social identity to be used in case of need. A
man can use only one identity at once but the one he puts to use
changes according to the community he is in—hence the title of this
book.

The concept *kahangi* is most frequently defined in Malaysia as
adik-beradik, brother and brother, and about half my informants
added that it referred to father's side only. The term which most
often replaces *kahangi* is *pupu*, but the Mandailingers point out that
this term, if used as a replacement for *kahangi*, must refer to father's
side only.[5] In only one Mandailing community in Malaysia are the
members of the lineage said explicitly to work together on the wet-
rice fields and in making gardens. In other communities, the concept
kahangi although known to older men has lost its function.

Among the Mandailingers in Malaysia the concept *mora* has
been used to express the differences of rank characteristic of Malay
life. The essence of the relationship between *mora* and *anak boru*,
i.e. the payment of respect from the latter to the former, has been
abstracted and the term has come to be defined as referring to *raja*,
i.e. indigenous leaders, or to persons of rank (*orang pangkat* or *yang
mulia*). Nevertheless, the wife-giving functions of one's *mora* are
recognized in some villages and the term is said to have been used in
marriage arrangements before World War II. The term *anak boru* is
known in some villages to mean "those who must marry with us" or
who are in our debt (*siperutang*) but where it is known at all, it is
known only to a few elders. The four terms belong together in that
they refer to related parts of the indigenous Mandailing social
system, but in Malaysia they do not all survive equally well. The
term *kahangi* is known in 95 per cent of communities, *marga* in 81
per cent, *mora* in 67 per cent and *anak boru* in 33 per cent. Moreover
the terms disappear in the order: *anak boru*; *mora*; *marga*; and
kahangi.[6] Later I shall make some inferences from this order about
processes of culture change.

The four terms survive in all villages in which Traditional Mandailing terminology is used. *Kahangi* and *marga* survive in all villages using a Generalized Sumatran terminology but *mora* and *anak
boru* fare less well. They survive better in wet-rice using villages than

they do in rubber-dominated villages. In a number of villages using Neo-Malayan terminology *marga* or both *marga* and *kahangi* are unknown. In wet-rice villages the terms survive better than they do in rubber-dominated villages.

The changes described above in kinship terminology and the membership of the larger kinship groups show that the wife-giving, wife-receiving relationships of traditional Mandailing society have been modified in Malaya. This in turn implies changes in the traditional forms of marriage. We shall now examine these changes.

Marriage

I asked my informants whether they preferred a young man to take a wife from the side of his father or the side of his mother. In twelve villages a preference was stated for mother's side; in two for father's side; and in five villages it was said that there was no preference for either side. Among those with a preference for mother's side the preference was held with different degrees of strength: some said that while they preferred a mother's-side marriage, marriage with either side was possible and one followed the wishes of the young people concerned; others, mainly those who said that marriage with mother's brother's daughter was the best kind of marriage, said that marriage on father's side was not allowed. One informant said that marriage to father's sister's daughter was like the earth creating the sky. In some villages in which there was a preference for mother's side it was pointed out that while customary law preferred that type of marriage, Islamic canon law allowed marriage with father's brother's daughter. In short, in villages in which Islam prevails over customary law there is a stated preference for marriage on father's side, in other villages there is a stated preference for marriage on mother's side or no preference. These alternatives are the known possible ways of acting; I shall now describe the way in which people act in practice.[7]

Marriage between relatives (48 per cent of all marriages) is much commoner in traditional wet-rice growing villages than it is in other villages (14 per cent). Marriage with mother's brother's daughter still occurs with sizeable frequency in the former (11 per cent), but less often in the latter. The relationships between partners in actual marriages do not contravene the idea of any village, but what is meant by preference for marriage on mother's side must be interpreted as including marriage with mother's sister's daughter as well as marriage with mother's brother's daughter.

Fig. 6. Percentage of marriages with Mandailingers and percentage of marriages within the village, for villages of different type

Village Type	% of Marriages with Mandailingers	% of Marriages within Village
Traditional wet-rice	90	57
Non-traditional wet-rice	25	25
Rubber	22	20

The members of the traditional wet-rice growing villages marry in such a way as to preserve the Mandailing identity of the village; 90 per cent of all marriages are with Mandailingers. Moreover, the number of marriages within the village (57 per cent) is also high. On the other hand in the non-traditional wet-rice villages only 25 per cent of marriages are with Mandailingers and only 25 per cent of marriages are within the village. The corresponding figures for rubber-dominated villages are 22 per cent and 20 per cent.[8] (See figure 6.)

The traditional Mandailing sleeping arrangements for young people and the courtship patterns that go with them are almost extinct in Malaysia. In one or two of the traditionalist Mandailing communities nubile girls sleep in the house of an old woman and youths sleep in the prayer house. In some other places the girls do not regularly gather in one house but youths sleep in the mosque or prayer house; and in the rest both girls and youths sleep in their own home. Courtship with the flute has almost disappeared. As one older commentator put it, "Times are changing—formerly we never saw the girl before the wedding, now a youth doesn't ask permission of the girl's father before they are off to the picture theatre."

But although youths have seized this greater freedom to meet, this has not made marriage any easier to arrange. The permission of a girl's *wali*, guardian, is necessary before she can marry. If permission is refused the only court to which appeal can be made, it is said, is the state ruler. If a *wali* is not available, the local *Penghulu* can stand in his place and supply a letter authorizing the marriage. If permission cannot be got the couple can run away and ask a religious judge to marry them, but this is difficult to arrange. Twenty years ago a youth who was very keen to marry a girl might have forced the situation by a surrender, *menyerah*, marriage. He would have gone to the girl's house with a sword (*kris*) and a white cloth and demanded that he be given the girl's hand or be killed by her family with the *kris* (the white cloth was to wrap his body in).[9] But such dramatic action is not now in vogue. A much easier way is to tempt the girl's father by offering a large bride-price.

When a couple have agreed to marry, the normal way to arrange the wedding is for the father of the youth to approach the father of the girl and ask for his permission in principle for the marriage to take place. The next step is a formal visit with presents from the youth's relatives who ask what form the wedding ceremony will take and how much the marriage portion will be (*pinang-meminang*). The latter is handed over in return for a promise from the girl's father to arrange the wedding on a certain date. My informants emphasize that nowadays the elders do not decide who shall marry whom, but they obviously have some control over their children through the important roles they play in arranging and carrying out the wedding.

In Malaysia the amount to be paid as *mahar* is regulated by the government. The Department of Religion fixes the amount to be paid from time to time in accordance with current social and economic conditions and the sultan issues a decree. Although the amounts vary from state to state the principle of government regulation introduces some uniformity within villages and fixes the minimum costs of a marriage.

Two kinds of payments are recognized in all Mandailing communities: *belanja tuboh*, literally, body payment; and *belanja angus*. The former is also called *emas kawin*, marriage gold, and is equated with *mahar*. According to the government regulations the amount to be paid varies from one social grade to another.[10] The villagers recognize the principle that the amount to be paid should be the same as the amount paid to the mother of the bride when the latter was wed. In some villages it is believed that the *belanja tuboh* must be paid in cash, in others that it can remain as a debt. The attitude of the Department of Religion in some areas, it is said, is that the *mahar* can remain as a debt for three months. According to Islamic law the *mahar* can remain as a debt for a period much longer so a man who cannot raise the money will let it remain as a debt for three months and then discuss the matter with his wife and the officials; alternatively, if he can borrow the money he can give it to his wife and she, if she wants to help him, can return it to him.

The second kind of universally recognized payment is *belanja angus*, or *belanja antaran*, delivery payment.[11] This is paid to the girl's father two weeks or more before the wedding and is supposed to be used as a contribution towards the cost of the wedding feast. Gifts (*pemberian*) made to the girl herself can be added to it.

Fig. 7. Mean amounts of marriage portion for marriages of different kinds

(The data are arranged for within-village marriages and between-village marriages, by Mandailing/Mandailing, Mandailing man/Other group woman, and Mandailing women/Other group man, by village type. The figures are mean amounts in Malaysian dollars.)

	Within Village	Between Village
M man/M woman		
Mand.-dominated village	36	475
Other wet-rice village	241	400
Rubber-dominated village	340	533
M man/Other group woman		
Mand.-dominated village	–	333
Other wet-rice village	445	488
Rubber-dominated village	–	654
M woman/M man		
Mand.-dominated village	–	467
Other wet-rice village	–	383
Rubber-dominated village	–	–
M woman/Other group man		
Mand.-dominated village	–	–
Other wet-rice village	238	371
Rubber-dominated village	433	605

Runaway marriages are rare and the following analysis of marriage payments will therefore concentrate on the type of marriage which is everywhere the norm, i.e. the proposal marriage. The *emas kawin* (*mahar*) in this type of marriage is a fixed cost, but there are wide variations, from nil to M$1,100, in the amount of the marriage portion (*belanja angus*). In one or two villages the amount paid for the wedding of a nubile girl may be fixed but in the others it varies by an order of about two. Thus the variation in any particular village in the amount paid is not nearly as great as the variation among all villages. The mean amounts paid for marriages of different kinds are shown in figure 7.

It is much cheaper from a man's point of view to marry within the village. This is especially true in the traditional villages where the ratio of wedding costs is one for a within-village marriage to twelve for a between-village marriage, less true in the non-traditional wet-rice growing villages and least true in the rubber-dominated villages. It is also cheaper for a Mandailinger to marry a Mandailing woman (except for men in traditional villages who take a Mandailing bride from outside the village). The highest payments are made in rubber-dominated villages and the lowest in traditional villages. Clearly to keep costs down a man should live in a traditional village, choose a Mandailing bride, and marry within the village; if he wants to choose his bride from a wider range, he must expect to pay more in wedding costs.

Post-wedding visits enable the newly married to keep in touch with their relatives; they have a cathartic effect and ease the transition into new roles. But post-marriage residence determines which group will have the services of the in-marrying, e.g. in traditional Mandailing culture in Sumatra a woman joins her husband and becomes part of the work force on the husband's family fields. This pattern survives in Traditional Mandailing communities in Malaysia. Ideally the couple stay with the youth's father for one year. In most other communities the couple live in the girl's father's house, but the period they spend there varies from a year or more to three days. The latter is the shortest possible time the couple can with propriety spend in the girl's father's house. It is really a post-wedding visit which may be symbolic of post-wedding residence, but which does not of course have the same economic advantages for the host household. The general norm in villages which practise this kind of post-wedding residence is to make an extended visit of one to three months to the bride's father's house and for the couple to then live wherever they choose. In three villages it is said that the couple prefer to live in their own house immediately after the wedding. In practice they make the customary post-wedding visits.

There is considerable variation within villages in the practices actually adopted. Pragmatic considerations are often the main determinants; as one informant put it, "we go wherever there is food available". There is widespread knowledge in Mandailing communities of the Mandailing tradition, but here, informants say, we follow *adat semondo*, the customary law of this country. Precept and practice do not always coincide.

In practice a man expects to pay more if he takes his bride off to live in town after the wedding. This is common in rubber-dominated villages, but rare in traditional villages. In the latter the most common practice is to live after the wedding in the house of the groom's father (67 per cent) or to live independently in the groom's father's village. In other wet-rice growing villages, to live in the groom's father's house is rare (7 per cent) but to live in the girl's father's house is common (70 per cent). Men in rubber-dominated villages go less frequently to live in their wife's father's house (40 per cent) and often live independently (55 per cent).

In short, the Mandailing tradition of post-wedding residence in the youth's father's house has been changed for residence in the girl's father's house, probably under Menangkabau influence, or in the couple's own house. The economic concerns which determine residence in practice are not those of the larger kin groups, but are related to the survival of the new nuclear family.

The proposal type of marriage takes into account the wishes of the couple, the wishes of their parents and relatives, public opinion within the village, and the requirements of Islamic canon law. Marriages can also be brought about in other ways in which one or more of these elements is disregarded. Runaway marriage (*kawin lari*) is recognized in about one-third of villages, but in other villages it is said not to be allowed or not to occur. The couple must go at least 115 kilometres from the girl's village before an Islamic judge will marry them without a letter from the girl's guardian. Runaway marriage is said to be shameful and the couple have to stay away from the village for some time; but it is certainly cheap. An unmarried girl and youth caught making love may be hauled before an Islamic judge and forced to marry. This so-called capture marriage (*kawin tangkap*) is known in most villages. In one community a *haji* who is a self-appointed guardian of the public morals and well known for keeping an eye on young couples is jokingly referred to as the "capture expert" (*tukang tangkap*). Abduction marriage in the traditional Mandailing sense is known in a few villages but apparently does not occur. Finally, according to the law of the land, civil marriage, i.e. marriage without the *nikah* ceremony, is possible and costs only M$10, but I was told that in Selangor at least the sultan would not tolerate civil marriage of Muslims.

It is apparent that the concept of the Great Gold (see p. 36) has disappeared among the Mandailingers in Malaysia. The principle of social grading which it exemplified has been incorporated in the graded payments for *mahar*. But the principle of fixed asymmetrical relations between groups and the notion of debt in perpetuity have been lost. The concept of the Little Gold has also disappeared although the *belanja angus* is paid in the same way and for the same purpose. It is recognized that according to Islamic law the *mahar* should be paid to the girl herself. In one traditional Mandailing village it is paid to the girl's father, i.e. is identified with the Little Gold. This is the last relic of the Little Gold idea.

The present payments lend themselves to the expression of social differences through the scale of the wedding feast. They are conclusive, i.e. they don't entail any repayment at a future time, although a young man must still visit his bride's parents.

Marriage element clustering

Some of the cultural elements related to marriage cluster together. Request marriage is found everywhere, and cannot be used to differentiate one village from another.[12] The recognized kinds of payments are also the same in all villages, but certain kinds of marriage preferences and post-wedding residence are associated with one another and with other cultural features. Girls' sleeping houses are found only in the traditional Mandailing villages. In four out of five of the villages with Traditional Mandailing kinship terminology a preference is expressed specifically for mother's brother's daughter marriage and these are the only villages in which the newly married reside with the youth's family. All the villages with a Generalized Sumatran kinship terminology except one prefer to marry on the mother's side of the family and favour residence with the girl's parents after marriage.[13] None of the villages using the Neo-Malayan type kinship terminology, however, favour marriage on the mother's side and the majority allow marriage on both sides (one village favours father's side). Moreover these villages favour a short period of residence in the girl's father's house followed by neolocal residence or neolocal residence after the "compulsory" three-day visit to the wife's parents. In short the decreasing importance of patriliny and the increasing importance of bilateral organization which characterize changes in the kinship terminology are found also in aspects of marriage.

Divorce

Ways of getting a divorce, because they are not institutionalized in traditional Mandailing culture, are not a good index of cultural change among Mandailingers in Malaysia.[14] But a change in attitudes to divorce might be brought about during the period of adaptation to the Malaysian social scene and this change would be reflected in a change in divorce rates. We shall look at divorce from this point of view. The traditional Mandailing attitude was that divorce should be prevented by strenuous efforts on the part of the relatives of the parties who met together to discuss any differences that had arisen. The Mandailingers held this attitude, I believe, because if a divorce took place, well-established woman-giving, woman-receiving relationships might be disrupted. Older men in some Mandailing communities in Malaysia echo this attitude; as one of them put it, "We Mandailingers don't want divorce in life, only in death" (*Kita orang Mandailing tidak mau cherai hidup, mau cherai mati saja*). Other culture groups in Malaya and Singapore have less stringent attitudes; Singapore Malays, for example, "hope that the [marriage] union will be permanent, but are fully aware of a strong possibility of its ending in divorce" (Djamour 1959, p. 130), and among Jelebu Malays "the villagers' amused attitudes show that there is not the slightest condemnation felt towards divorce as long as the parting is managed without unseemly discord and emotion" (Swift 1965, p. 121). We might have expected the Mandailingers to adopt these attitudes in the course of time, especially when they lived in close contact with other groups and intermarried with them.

In fact the divorce rate varies from village to village.[15] In the traditional wet-rice growing villages it is generally low and averages 5 per cent; in non-traditional wet-rice growing villages it ranges from nil to 22 per cent and averages 10 per cent; and in rubber-dominated villages it ranges from nil to 42 per cent and averages 19 per cent. In short, in villages in which the most common type of marriage is Mandailinger with Mandailinger, and post-wedding residence is in the village, the divorce rate is low; in villages in which Mandailing/ Mandailing marriages account for about one-quarter of all marriages and post-wedding residence is usually in the village the rate is moderate; and in villages in which the predominant type of marriage is a marriage outside the village with a partner from another culture group, the rate is highest.

Divorce is apparently not controlled by economic factors because the rate is higher in rubber-dominated villages in which marriages are most expensive to arrange. Residence in these villages is predominantly neolocal; the families of the partners therefore do not lose labour when the divorce takes place, but on the contrary are likely to gain labour from the return of the divorced partners. They have nothing to lose by not opposing the divorce. The greater mobility of the newly married also contributes to divorce, because a woman who is taken away from her kin has less chance of calling on them for support in quarrels with her husband.

It seems reasonable to conclude that the rate of divorce is a function of attitudes to divorce which are related to the degree of social disruption which a divorce causes.

Inheritance

Inheritance according to Islamic canon law (*hukum firait*), which is the officially sanctioned system, sometimes differs from inheritance according to village customary law. If an estate is officially divided the *Penghulu* investigates the affair and the division is made by the collector of inland revenue according to Islamic canon law. There is a distinction in the villager's minds between division by the collector and division by agreement among inheritors (known as the *waris*). There are differences in custom from village to village. In traditional Mandailing culture the inheritance is divided among the male heirs; in Perak customary law sons receive three times as much as daughters;[16] according to Tolu customary law (the Tolu are an immigrant Sumatran group) sons receive "a little more" than daughters; and in some villages it is the custom for sons and daughters to receive equal shares. The contrast between matrilineal inheritance and their own system is recognized by the villagers of the Mandailing enclave in Negeri Sembilan. The Negeri Sembilan people, they say, use Islamic canon law to divide rubber gardens and customary law for the house, *dusun*, and wet-rice fields. Of their own system, the Mandailing system as they see it, they say, "If I have land at present, then my boys use it, I can't say to them, 'Don't use this inheritance'; we use the land together. We discuss among ourselves; this is our way. While I am alive, they can use it, but they can't sell it; when I die, if they want to sell it they can do so. Of course if my son wants to go ahead on his own, open the forest, say, and make a garden, I don't interfere, that is his business." All these customs contrast with Islamic canon law according to which the inheritance is divided in fixed proportions and sons receive twice as much as daughters.

To avoid dividing up the property according to Islamic canon law various stratagems are adopted. The first is for a man to distribute his property before his death. In this way he can give more to his favourites, but he runs the risk of living on as a poor neglected father in old age: the second is to use a will (*wasiat*) in which Islamic canon law is circumvented. This may result in some inheritors trying to get a bigger share through litigation.[17] The third is for one person to receive the property intact and pay off the other inheritors; and the fourth is to keep the property intact and divide up the yield from it according to canon law. Land which is registered in the name of a single person, as all land on group settlement schemes must be, poses a special problem. If a man dies and the land is registered in his wife's name, then it will not be divided; if it is registered in his name, then officially the inheritance should be divided according to canon law, but only one person's name can appear in the register. The villager's way out is usually to not re-register the land but to divide it or the yield from it according to their own custom. The principle behind all these strategems is to avoid canon law being used instead of custom.

Another principle widely used is readjustment of the shares in or use of the inheritance among the inheritors according to need. Persons in well-paid jobs, like teachers, will not take their share of the inheritance, but give it to a needier relative. The clothes of a woman who dies are given to her daughters. The traditional Mandailingers living as an enclave in Negeri Sembilan say, "If we have a sister we, her brothers, look after her. If her husband comes to live in our village he can share in our inheritance as long as he stays. But if our sister goes away she can't take anything. She can leave if she wishes, but we shall look after the children, we feel responsibility for them. According to Negeri Sembilan customary law forty days after the death of a woman her husband has to leave. Then there are two deaths, the wife and the husband, and the children have no father. We think differently—if our sister's husband wants to stay here after her death he can do so and use her share of the inheritance; we think of our sister's children as ours." A similar principle is used in some Mandailing communities when a man dies—his widow acts as "guard" (*jaga*) for the property which remains undivided until her death, i.e. she has the use of it for herself and her dependent children.

These general principles are widespread, but the actual practice in inheritance differs from village to village. Islamic canon law is known everywhere and in some villages it is the only system used, in others it exists alongside other systems which are more often used in practice. In traditional wet-rice villages a woman always acts as "guard" for the property of her late husband; this practice is common also in other wet-rice growing communities, but is not mentioned in rubber-dominated villages. Equal division of the inheritance among the children of the deceased is mentioned in six villages. Four of these are villages in which Neo-Malayan kinship terminology is used.[18]

Magico-religious organization

Islamization was nominally complete in the Mandailing areas of Sumatra before the founders of most Mandailing communities in Malaya left. But Islamic doctrine and worship existed alongside pre-Islamic magic and medicine, which were in process of translation into an Islamic idiom. Thus medicines formerly used for exorcising spirits (*gebiah*) and ritual drums (*gebang*) were used for getting rid of *jihin*.[19] The range of spirit types included Batak and Islamic forms.

Islamic sacrificial rituals such as those carried out at the birth of a child (*kekah*), and the breaking of the fast (*korban*) were introduced.

The practical tasks of the medicine men and the religious experts included medical care, exorcising ghosts and spirits, foretelling the future, ensuring the growth of crops, and carrying out rites of passage. In the different economic and social context of Malaya some elements of this syncretic religious system were strengthened, others were lost and replaced. (See plate 3.)

Ghosts and spirits are no longer dominant forces (in spite of the important place in the indigenous Malay belief system which Winstedt [1951] gives them). The Sumatran concepts of non-*jihin* spirits, and the evil spirits of murdered persons are unknown in present-day Mandailing communities in Malaysia. Drums are now used only at marriage ceremonies in some wet-rice villages (they are not mentioned in rubber-dominated villages). Experts in dream interpretation and divination are no longer found and even the practice of visiting the graves of holy men (*keramat*) for the purpose of obtaining some future benefit has declined in recent years and is almost extinct in rubber-dominated villages.[20] The ritual of the rice-fields, including the turning in of the stalks of the ripened grain in order to preserve the spirit of the rice, is carried out only by old men in a few villages. On the other hand, the magical care of the sick still flourishes. The medicine man who is in touch with a special helpful spirit has disappeared (presumably because of changes in knowledge of the etiology of disease) but the ordinary medicine man is common in both wet-rice and rubber-dominated villages. The singing of Islamic religious songs with a drum accompaniment (*dikir ulu*) which affords an exciting religious experience is now rare in Mandailing communities, and there has been a decline in recent years in both wet-rice growing and rubber-dominated villages in religious sacrifice. Religious education, on the other hand, has become more organized. There are three types of teachers: those who are paid by the government and visit villages within an area once to four times a month; unofficial teachers who are given gifts (*sedekah*) by those they teach; and religious teachers in public schools. Some villages have no visits from official teachers; formal religious education appears to be more highly organized in rubber-dominated villages than it is in wet-rice growing villages.

In summary, the Sumatran elements in the syncretic magico-religious system which the Mandailing founding fathers brought with them have almost completely disappeared. They were not replaced, except possibly in the field of medicine, by indigenous Malay magic and the field was thus left open for the development of Islam. But in recent years Islamic ritual has itself declined. As one informant put it, "people are satisfied with the elements they get in school, they don't know anything about deeper things".

Plate 3. Village affairs: older men carry out prayers for a new-born child

Plate 4. Village affairs: younger men led by a headman discuss village development

Conclusion

Three variables have been related to culture change in this and the previous chapter: type of economy; composition of the village population; and type of social organization. Villages have been divided first into wet-rice growing and rubber-dominated villages; second, among wet-rice growing villages those in which the Mandailingers comprise 86 per cent or more of the population have been separated as traditional villages; and third the non-traditional and rubber-dominated villages have been divided according to the kinship terminology in use. Thus we have a fivefold typology of villages: traditional; non-traditional/Generalized Sumatran; non-traditional/Neo-Malayan; rubber-dominated/Generalized Sumatran; and rubber-dominated/Neo-Malayan. The pattern of features found in the traditional villages is fairly clear cut and will be described below; the main task of this conclusion is to describe and account for the concomitant changes in various fields of culture that took place as the Mandailingers substituted rubber production for wet-rice production. This substitution took place abruptly in some communities when they left Sumatra and landed in Malaya, in others it was brought about gradually by economic pressures from the environment.

Traditional villages

If we imagine the use of traditional practices in all fields of village life as forming scales from high use to low use, then the traditional villages will be at the high end of all scales. They have the highest rate of Mandailing language use; one has the traditional Mandailing division of labour on the rice-fields and the others show minimal change; all have Traditional Mandailing kinship terminology; the four key social group terms are known to older men; they have the highest rate of within-village marriage, of marriage between Mandailinger and Mandailinger, and the highest difference in costs between a within-village marriage and a between-village marriage; they are the only villages with girls' sleeping houses; with preference for marriage with mother's brother's daughter, and in which residence after the wedding is normally in the house of the groom's father. All these practices accord with traditional Mandailing practice in Sumatra.

But these practices do not of themselves constitute an effective asymmetrical marriage system. The building blocks for such a system are lineage units (*kahangi*) and there is no evidence of the existence of the latter as corporate social groups in these communities. The rice fields are divided up into small individually owned units, whereas in an effective lineage system one would expect that they would be divided into corporately owned parcels. Moreover, some young men do not know to which clan they belong, so that it is unlikely that the principle of clan exogamy exerts much effect in marriage choice. On the other hand, status differentiation within the village is along traditional lines: the heads of four out of the five traditional villages are descendants of *raja* lines. All leaders are accorded a good deal of respect, have a faithful following, and spend a long time in office.[21] Traditions, including the tradition of mutual help among relatives in production, survive in these villages because the mass of members entrust the running of villages affairs to their knowledgeable leaders, as they did in the past. Three of these villages survived as enclaves in Negeri Sembilan and two under the protection of their own *Penghulu* in an area in which the rice fields escaped large-scale destruction by tin mining.

The transition from wet-rice to rubber

In non-traditional wet-rice growing villages the agricultural subsistence complex of Sumatra survived, but the division of labour in production is not in terms of clear-cut roles for men and women but in terms of cooperation. This is a pointer to other changes, in the first place to a change in the economic units within the village. In traditional Mandailing culture these were extended families with a core of close patrikin, whereas the economic unit is now the nuclear family. Second, cooperation is indicative of the changed status of women: in traditional culture their transfer from group to group created symbolic ties between groups, though in practice they functioned as a source of labour for the rice fields; in Malaysia they have become nuclear family partners. Third, the structure of work groups has changed: in traditional culture male or female tasks requiring more than one person were done by calling on close relatives of the appropriate sex; in Malaysia the work group can consist of both men and women, and the basic work group consists of a man and his wife. Finally, these changes are indicative of a transformation from a kinship system dominated by patrilineages of different span to a bilateral system in which kinship is reckoned through both men and women.

But as we have seen, both Generalized Sumatran and Neo-Malayan terminology occur in non-traditional villages and in rubber-dominated villages. For the moment I shall regard these two systems of terminology as representing alternative courses for social change. Whichever course is adopted the concepts for wife-giving and wife-receiving social units and sometimes also the concepts for the larger social units are lost. These losses occur more often in rubber-dominated villages in which the system of production does not call for joint action among relatives, but also occur in villages in which the Neo-Malayan system of terminology is used. In our analysis of marriage practices we must therefore take into account both the type of terminology and the system of production.

Marriage with relatives occurs more often in Generalized Sumatran villages than it does in Neo-Malayan villages, but in Generalized Sumatran villages marriage within the village is now slightly less common than it is in Neo-Malayan villages. These relationships hold for both non-traditional wet-rice growing villages and rubber-dominated villages. In any kind of village wedding, costs are less for a within-village marriage than they are for a between-village marriage. In villages with a Generalized Sumatran terminology the wedding costs are less than they are in the corresponding village with a Neo-Malayan terminology, but in rubber-dominated villages this difference is less. Overall, wedding costs are higher in rubber-dominated villages, in which there is more spare cash, than they are in corresponding villages of any type.

Post-wedding residence in non-traditional/Generalized Sumatran villages which is predominantly with the bride's father contrasts with post-wedding residence in traditional villages which is with the groom's father. In non-traditional/Neo-Malayan villages on the other hand, although residence with the bride's father is the commonest form, residence with the groom's father also occurs (15 per cent). In non-traditional/Generalized Sumatran villages the post-wedding residence is the same as in the rubber-dominated/Generalized Sumatran villages, but the pattern in non-traditional/Neo-Malayan villages is very different from the pattern in rubber-dominated/Neo-Malayan villages. In the latter greater freedom of choice plus the greater availability of cash lead to marked emigration and independent residence. Those who do not emigrate choose to live with the bride's father or with the groom's father in about equal numbers. This is the situation one might expect in a society with a bilateral system of kinship terminology.

One final question remains: why were Generalized Sumatran terminology and its associated practices generated in some villages and Neo-Malayan and its associated features in others? The traditional villages are relatively small, but have a high percentage of Mandailingers so that the size of the Mandailing community is about the same in all villages. Percentage of Mandailingers in village types other than traditional does not differ significantly from one type to another. We are left with village composition as a variable which may possibly be associated with type of terminology. The percentage of indigenous Malays is lower in non-traditional/Generalized Sumatran villages than it is in non-traditional/Neo-Malayan villages; the percentage is markedly lower in rubber/Generalized Sumatran villages than it is in rubber/Neo-Malayan villages. The percentage of other Sumatrans is fairly constant in village types other than rubber/Neo-Malayan, but in the latter it falls to a much lower figure. The ratio of indigenous Malays to other Sumatrans is as follows:

NONTRAD/GS   16/22
NONTRAD/NM   25/29
RUBBER/GS   8/23
RUBBER/NM   21/13

There is therefore a tendency for the percentage of indigenous Malays to increase in Neo-Malayan villages and in rubber/Neo-Malayan villages they outnumber other Sumatrans. The conclusion one can draw is that contact with indigenous Malays has led to adoption of a Neo-Malayan terminology.

This concludes our review of changes in the culture of Mandailing communities brought about through accommodation to economic and social realities at the local level and we turn now to look at attempts made by the Malaysian government to change Mandailing identity through administrative action.

PART TWO

Nation building : the formal context of Malayanization

The basic steps

Immediately after the Japanese surrender the Communists tried to take over the administration of Malaya. Their temporary control was based on the guerrilla forces which were mainly Chinese and which killed a number of persons alleged to have favoured the Japanese. The Communists spread the rumour that an army from China was coming to their support, and fights between Malays and Chinese broke out in the western states.

The growing self-consciousness of the Malays was evident in their opposition to the British proposal of 1945 for a Malayan Union which would have reversed the pre-war trend to decentralization, severely reduced the power and prestige of the sultans, and reduced the status of the Malays by granting citizenship equally to all races. The Federation Agreement of 1948, which confirmed the pre-war privileges of the sultans, was more in line with Malay sentiments.[1]

The Communists, having failed in their take-over bid, tried to prevent the economic recovery and political development of Malaya under the British by guerrilla activity during the period known in Malaya as the Emergency (1948-60).[2]

The Emergency stimulated cooperation between the Malay ruling class and elements of the Chinese and Indian commercial class who were in favour of independence from Britain and as a result of their joint efforts Malaya became an elective monarchy within the British Commonwealth in 1957. These events sensitized all groups in Malaya to the idea of Malayan citizenship. But independence was achieved without creating a dramatic aura of revolution and sacrifice. Therefore during the period of Indonesian Confrontation of the new Malaysia (the union of Malaya and the British territories in northern Borneo) the Malaysian administration had a hard job trying to deepen the national consciousness of the common people.

This rally-round-the-flag exercise was not successful so far as recent Sumatran immigrants to West Malaysia were concerned,[3] but Confrontation, which lasted from 1963 to 1966, did cut the link between Sumatra and Malaya which had continued to exist in de facto economics owing to Chinese and Malayan smuggling across the Straits. During Confrontation the Indonesian element of the population kept quiet about their origins, but as soon as it was over they began to think again about visiting their homeland.

The attempt by the Malaysian government to unite the races of the nation could only put a gloss on racial biases built into the federal constitution, e.g. the strong preference to be given to Malays in recruitment and promotion in the administration (nominally for ten years) and the use of Malay as the national language. The last became the centre point of conflict between Chinese and Malay students at the University of Malaya, Kuala Lumpur, in 1963, and has continued to be a central issue in Malay-Chinese relations. Nevertheless, the Malaysian government has pushed on with its programme for promoting the Malay language and has in the last five years had considerable success in transforming the language environment in West Malaysian cities.[4] Relationships between Chinese and Malays in the countryside have continued as an economic symbiosis disrupted by occasional acts of group violence like the Pangkor incident.[5] Until recently the government did not take positive steps to build new cross-racial relationships but was content to stop the spread of violence. The committees for racial harmony which exist at the local level in the western states of West Malaysia still meet only after an outbreak of violence. Thus the possibility of racial conflict must be taken into account by every Malay when he accesses his life chances and those of his children in West Malaysia.

Local power and resources

Having beaten the Communists, got rid of the British and taken charge of the new nation, the ruling Alliance Party[6] set about demonstrating the attractions of citizenship to the rural population, through the decision-making system at the local level. This contains elements of the old and the new. The all-powerful district officer is an inheritance from the British system of administration developed in the Federated Malay States; his counterpart, the sultan's representative who is known in Perak as Orang Besar Jajahan, is responsible for Muslim religious affairs, and a third party poised in potential opposition to the district officer is the elected member of parliament.

The government has made strong efforts since Federation to provide more facilities and economic opportunities in the countryside. The effort of will and most of the money for the rural development programme has come since Federation from the central government at Kuala Lumpur. Centrally determined are the rationale and mode of operation of the programme which is run in the same way in all districts. The success of the programme however at the local level turns on the energy and knowledge of local officials, available resources and the motivations of farmers.

The set of historically derived political and administrative structures provides a common context for all Mandailing communities. The territorial chiefs, or O.B.J.s as they are called in Perak and Selangor, have no formal power although they are the sociological descendants of the once all-powerful local chiefs whose word meant life or death to the peasants. They are appointed by the sultan as his representative. Most of them are older men on a pension, but some are only thirty years old. The office is not hereditary, but in Perak because it is often filled by members of old Perak families successive incumbents are likely to be related to one another and to pursue a common policy. They are supposed to be consulted by the administration in matters concerning the Islamic religion. Effective authority associated with this position is epitomized in the saying "as windy as an O.B.J." Some sultan's representatives however are finding a new role and avenue of influence as members of development committees.

The power lost by the local chiefs has been gained by the officers of the administration in a form hedged about, of course, by rule and regulation, but backed by wide authority. The backbone of the administration is the hierarchy of officers—chief secretary, district officer, assistant district officer, *Penghulu* and village head—who form the "line" officers of this bureaucracy. Staff officers attached to state headquarters, district and sometimes sub-district offices have specialized functions such as irrigation, agriculture, and public works. Planning, allocation of resources, and supervision of activities are supposed to be carried out at each level by the line officers concerned.

Whereas the O.B.J. often carries on his business in his own house which is no larger or better than that of any other fairly well-off person, the district officer presides over a complex of offices occupying a large building in a prominent position in the regional centre.[7] Even the sub-district office is often the largest building in the local town, being about on a par with the school. To the average villager, the district or sub-district office symbolizes the source of effective local power.[8]

But that power comes into contact with the life of the villager through the *Penghulu*. Formerly *Penghulu* were appointed by and represented the sultan, and the office remained in one family. The incumbent had frequent contact with the villagers and exercised a permanent, mild supervision over village affairs in a small area called a *mukim*. Nowadays, *Penghulu* are firmly part of the administrative bureaucracy. A school certificate is required for entry to the *Penghulu* service which is graded and attracts fifteen to twenty applicants for each vacancy.[9] Some *Penghulu*, instead of being generalists, act as assistants at the district office for special matters such as development. Newly-appointed *Penghulu* are liable to be transferred to a new area every two or three years. But there are many older *Penghulu* who have been in the job in the same area for many years. Most *Penghulu* live in a better-than-average house, near to their *balai*, an open-sided meeting place and office, but not in the village. Some *Penghulu* are entitled to hold a *Penghulu* court and can inflict a fine of up to M$25. In a large *mukim* there may be up to four *Penghulu* working under a senior *Penghulu*. There is a distinct quality of independence about the members of the *Penghulu* service, which is even more marked in Negeri Sembilan where the *Penghulu* is regarded as the upholder of customary law. Some long-established *Penghulu* who are indigenous to and have lived in an area much longer than the district officer and his assistants are "little kings" in their own *mukim*.

The role of village head, *Ketua Kampong*, is undergoing the same kind of change as the role of *Penghulu*, a change from familistic, father figure and protector to administrator. There are a few older heads of Mandailing communities whose names were put forward as a single candidate and were confirmed by the sultan in an office they have occupied for up to thirty years. They still operate in the old way. But the village heads who have taken office recently have been elected, or selected by the administration from a short list of candidates put forward by the village. These heads remain in office for four or five years. Moreover the units over which these heads have jurisdiction, instead of being the small homogeneous community, well-knit by kinship and economic ties, contain several subcultural groups and sometimes four or five distinct communities. Unofficial boundaries between these units are recognized by the people and sometimes each unit has a *pengurusi*, or organizer who acts as an assistant village head. The effective influence of a village head may therefore be confined to that part of his area of jurisdiction within which he lives.

In some townships in which Mandailingers live the functions of the *Penghulu* and village head are performed by a local council whose members are usually elected.[10] The chairman of the council may be a non-Malay. The council gets an income from taxes on house sites, business sites and night soil collection and lets contracts for jobs like cleaning the streets and collecting rubbish. The income of a small council may be of the order of M$25,000 per annum. Some district officers see the councils as experiments in democracy and some would like to have the power to nominate the chairman.

The "politician" is a rising power figure on the rural scene. The rural Malays are becoming more democracy conscious and familiar with democratic processes. The local member of parliament symbolizes the newly-realized power of the electors and they are liable to appeal to him for help. The member sees himself as an authority in "his" area. These ideas tend to put the local member of parliament in opposition to the district officer. There was a public confrontation between a district officer and a local member of parliament with both parties vying for popular support in Selangor in 1967. The district officer wanted to evict illegal squatters who were supported by the member of parliament and was forced to call a local press conference in order to make his views known. Wherever there is a power struggle of this kind the wants of the ordinary farmer are likely to be met.

Political and administrative functions

The guidelines of policy are laid down in Kuala Lumpur. Phrases or slogans of ministers which epitomise the policies of the government may be found on the walls of the operations room in the district office. The practice of administration is fairly uniform from state to state and district to district, but in style administration varies from district to district, *mukim* to *mukim*, and village to village according to the personality and experience of the relevant head and the composition of "his" population. (See plate 4.)

Economic development

The most important activity of the administration is promoting development. Birth, marriage, death, inheritance, and social control, the basic social processes of village life, are self-regulating; the administration has only to record the results. But these processes do not generate a desire for progress, which has to be stimulated by the administration through its own technical and social organs. Elaborate maps covering the past and future of all phases of the development programme and tables of expenditure are displayed in the operations room in the district office. There is a development map for the *mukim* in the *Penghulu's balai* and one for the village in the village hall. The district officer, his assistant *Penghulu* and members of special departments meet in the operations room once a week for discussions on development, and at the monthly village meetings the A.D.O. takes the opportunity to harangue the villagers about the need for self-help. As one district officer put it; "The main problem with development is to get people to do things for themselves. They expect to get everything from the government. Material things one can easily give, it is more difficult to change minds."

Political development

The actions of the government have created a climate of expectation which has turned development into a political arena at the local level. It was pointed out to me in 1968 that expenditure in certain development projects had increased because that was a pre-election year.[11] But apart from this vote-winning function development involves the district officer and the local politicians in a struggle for influence. The political pose adopted by most D.O.s and their assistants is that of enforcement officer. The law is on their side; they can open land, provide capital goods, and oversee their use according to law. The local politicians pose as the friend of the common man, to whom the same kind of appeal for protection can be made as was made to the sultan's representative in the past.

The struggle between D.O. and politician therefore becomes overt when enterprising citizens occupy land illegally. When the Emergency ended there was nothing to stop the Chinese from going back to rural areas and some did so as squatters in remote districts. But in addition, it is said, land-hungry Chinese occupy private land and become so belligerent that the owners are afraid of them. Houses go up overnight. The Chinese are uncooperative and uninformative in relations with administration and there are too few officers to control the situation. When a district officer regards illegal occupants of district land as a security risk and expels them he is likely to find himself ranged opposite the local politician.[12]

These situations of public confrontation have sharpened the public's appreciation of where the power lies and led to a growth of group self-consciousness: Malays versus Chinese and Indians; conservative and generally older Malays versus progressive and generally younger Malays; townsmen versus rural dwellers; wealthier Malays commanding educational opportunities versus not so wealthy Malays. At present some of these labels represent emergent categories which have not yet become collectivities. But others stand for nascent collectivities which are being mobilized by formal political parties; some townsmen for example have been taken over by the socialist party. Overarching other polarities is the Malay-Chinese antipathy, which is acerbated at present by the extension of Chinese agriculture. In this situation the administration, charged with administering the law, appears to the public to take on the old role of the British as Malay protector.

Land development schemes

The political aim of the rural development programme is to make as many rural dwellers as possible satisfied with the government. The programme has been implemented with vigour, especially since the First Malaysia Plan started in 1966.[13] But as far as its effect on the movement of the rural population, increasing per capita income, and raising the standard of living is concerned, the plan has two antipathetical elements: on the one hand improved amenities in the villages, which can be enjoyed by the rich and the poor alike, tend to keep people at home; on the other providing land distant from the village for the landless or near-landless tempts the poor to move out. In and around the villages major works, such as road making and dam building costing up to M$50,000, are sometimes carried out under the plan. For amenities within the village the village vote usually goes first to a new prayer house and then to electricity and water pipes. Other popular structures are badminton courts, clinics, and meeting halls. This expenditure on social capital makes the village a better place to live in but does not alter the social and economic relationships among the inhabitants, which turn upon rights over land.

The land development schemes are a source of both social change and social stability. The schemes are sponsored and financed by both the federal and state governments and are of three general types: fringe development, group settlement, and controlled alienation. The fringe development schemes encompass land near the village. The government clears the land, divides it into lots of one to one and a half hectares and provides the seed or plants, normally rubber, and fertilizer. The tenant works the land, under a temporary occupation licence at a small fixed rent,[14] and he receives the title to the land when the rubber is tapped.

The group settlement schemes are located some way away from existing communities. Each settler gets two and a half hectares of land for a permanent crop, usually rubber, and nearly one hectare for fruit trees and a house. The government provides tools, seed, and fertilizer, and pays a subsidy of about M$20 per month for the first year and M$10 per month for the second year. The agricultural work is supervised by a government officer under the controlled alienation *terkawal* scheme. The government specifies the crop to be grown, rubber or oil palm, but then gives only advice. The tenant works with his own tools and pays off the premium of about M$125 per hectare at the rate of M$3.75 per hectare per year for the first ten years and M$15 per hectare per year thereafter. He gets a 99-year title.

The fringe alienation schemes benefit both those who already own land in the village and those who do not. They supplement, or will in the future supplement, the productive capacity of the village, but do little to reduce the difference between those who have a little land and those who have a lot. The group settlement schemes are for the landless, and a participant must change his residence. From the government point of view the controlled alienation schemes are a cheaper form of group settlement scheme, but since no subsidy is paid they tend to benefit those who already have some capital on which they can live until the new plantings mature. They do not reduce the volume of local labour available for rubber tapping, because a landless man who takes part in the scheme must continue to earn a living until his own trees become tappable. In the short term both the fringe alienation and controlled alienation schemes have little effect on the relative socio-economic positions of persons within the village because there is a period of waiting while newly planted crops mature. The group settlement schemes however reduce the volume of landless labour in the village. In the long term the schemes should theoretically provide everyone with land of his own to work and there will be a shortage of labour for tapping. From the Malay peasant point of view the relative advantage of these schemes at the present time turns on a struggle between love of freedom from control and love of land ownership.

The land development schemes are administered by the district office. The mode of administration is formally clear cut, but in practice subject to local political pressures. Candidates for the group settlement schemes are interviewed by a board with members from Kuala Lumpur. The main criteria for selection are: landless; aged about thirty-five (the older and the younger get less land); experience as a farmer; other experience; and number of dependants. The local district office is usually allotted a proportion of places for a scheme which falls within its area. An applicant must take up his block as land becomes available. For the other schemes recommendation by the *Penghulu* carries a good deal of weight. The fringe alienation and controlled alienation lots are periodically inspected by an officer assigned to each scheme. Tenants whose progress in developing their lot is unsatisfactory are liable to be evicted and some evictions have been carried out by tough-minded district officers.

The administration has tried to meet the problems of special groups. In the Kuala Kangsar District for example there is a special development of 2,835 hectares for "the youth of all races". There are 200 settlers aged eighteen to twenty-three each of whom will get 10 hectares for planting oil palm. They live in a long-house, work communally, are paid M$15-20 per month for four years, and cannot marry. For the owners of old gardens with less than 4 hectares of rubber land there is a rubber replanting scheme subsidized by the government. Finally, the government often helps the Chinese by turning a blind eye on illegal squatters on government lands.

Official land schemes appear to favour Malays both in their setting and the selection of settlers. Some Chinese avoid the schemes because they wish to be free of government restriction and many squat on unused land and pay no rent following a practice which became widespread during the Japanese occupation. Most Chinese in rural areas however are associated with trade in market towns. The effect of the land development schemes on the distribution of the Malay population is to increase the size of the penumbra of utilized land around the established settlements and to create new nuclei of settlement with limited scope for expansion on the federal schemes.

From the government point of view there is political profit in making the rural development programme work by translating economic development into a form acceptable to the Malay villagers. The monthly village meetings which bring development at the grass roots constantly under review are a means of inducing the villagers to participate. Other means are demonstrations and handouts by agricultural stations,[15] regional agricultural shows, organized communal work sessions,[16] and inter-village competitions.[17]

The land development schemes are a source of social change in that they reduce the number of the landless and increase the holdings of the landed.[18] Everyone is pushed up the social ladder, the relative difference between rich and poor remains the same, but the sharp difference in cultural and economic terms between the landed and the landless disappears. The schemes are a source of social stability in that they provide satisfactions in a number of ways to a large number of people and the villagers have the feeling of living in a modernized milieu. Thus the schemes probably act as a brake on but do not entirely prevent migration to the towns. At the same time they provide new material for land dealing and absentee landlords are probably increasing in number on some schemes; in one district illegal "sales" of land on land schemes is being investigated. On one long-established wet-rice growing project in another district, illegal transfers of land for cash from "owner" to "owner" are a regular practice. No letter of transfer of ownership, or witnesses, are used and the name on the land register remains unchanged, but as far as practical Malay economics is concerned the land has been transferred. These practices will no doubt later increase in frequency on the newly developed areas. Hence the probable effects of the schemes will be, in sequence: reduction in the number of landless without reduction in the volume of labour available for tapping until the newly planted trees become tappable; reduction in the amount of labour available for tapping as people begin to tap their own; transfer of new gardens to others (mainly the well-established); and re-emergence of a landless minority. The stage already reached and the speed with which the stages will be reached vary from district to district depending on terrain, number of schemes, and the type of village economy established before development began. But whatever the outcome of these social and economic processes, from the point of view of Mandailing (and other Sumatran) immigrants in West Malaysia they do provide economic opportunities of the very sort that the ancestors of those migrants were looking for when they came to Malaysia; from the point of view of the Malaysian elite they are a means of engaging the migrant with the Malaysian polity: the problem for the government is how to entice the farmers to become willing subjects for social engineering.

Motivating the Malay farmer

The land utilization pattern of the Malays is a function of the liking of Malay farmers to be enfolded within an Islamic community and to own land for its own sake.[19] Unless landless they do not wish to move from their own settlement. Within the confines of their own settlement they like to acquire land but not necessarily to greatly increase production. However, since World War II there has been an increasing desire for relatively expensive goods such as motor cycles, television sets, and motorcars. The government tries to make these interests of individual Malays coincide with the national interest by rationalizing farming methods. Information about how to grow better crops is conveyed via the agricultural extension services of government and the Rubber Research Institute. At government-sponsored agricultural shows inter-village rivalry is promoted by presentation of prizes for health competitions and the like. A suitable order of speeches for such an occasion is: district officer, land development officer (with eulogies on double cropping), member of parliament, and high official from state headquarters. By exhortation, by example in the Agriculture Department garden, by demonstration of new machinery, and by encouraging the redistribution of capital through the formation of cooperatives, the ad-

Plate 5. Interiors: the kitchen of a growing family

Plate 6. Interiors: the contemporary living room of a successful farmer/businessman

ministration tries to increase the real income of rural Malays. The Rubber Research Institute supports these efforts by developing high yielding varieties of rubber trees and conducting extension courses on the growing of rubber. The net result is an increase in farming skills among Malays without any fundamental change in economic motivation, but with an increasing desire for more manufactured goods. (See plates 5 and 6.)

Outlets for ambition

Sumatran youths in their mid teens customarily travel outside their natal village for a year or two to seek their fortune. For this period of wander the child of a Sumatran immigrant in Malaysia can substitute as extended a stay in the academic system as his family can afford. This training is a prerequisite for a favourite Malay avenue to status, entry into government service, and entails a move to a large city (Kuala Lumpur or Penang). Thus the yield from the extra effort of the farmers is not reinvested in the countryside and the child loses his identification with the sub-cultural group of his father and becomes a man of the urban world. In the past a relatively large number of the sons of Mandailing migrants in West Malaysia has achieved this status. In recent years the Malaysian government has created other avenues through which ambitious youths can get ahead: technical training through the Mara Institute or local technical colleges; job opportunities in rurally located industries; and opportunities to take up land for growing cash crops. The social and cultural changes that these policies will engender will take place in the next ten years. What we shall now describe is the degree to which past experience has led the Mandailingers in Malaysia to take part in Malaysian affairs.

Mandailing involvement in Malaysian affairs

Introduction

Some Mandailingers search for security and economic success by making a short foray from their natal village, others wage a permanent overseas campaign. Some of these fortune hunters eventually become colonists and adjust to the cultural milieu in which they settle by encapsulation (like the traditional villages), by coordination of their efforts with those of other colonists, or by exploitation of opportunities offered by the host culture, but whatever they do they become involved to some degree in Malaysian affairs. In this chapter I shall explore two parts of this involvement: involvement in village affairs; and extra-village contacts.

Village affairs

Location in space

The social, political, and economic affairs of a large village are different from those of a small village. In a large village not all people see one another every day and public facilities such as prayer houses, wells, places for washing clothes, and coffee shops are duplicated and spread out so that there are several nuclei of social life in the village precincts. The distribution of the houses of persons who regard themselves as belonging to the same social group reflects the network of social and economic ties and can be used as an indicator of the social alignments within the village. In nineteenth century Mandailing villages in Sumatra the houses of men of the same clan were clustered together and the village was surrounded by a fence. In contemporary Mandailing villages in Sumatra patrilineal kinsmen still like to live close to one another and the village tends to

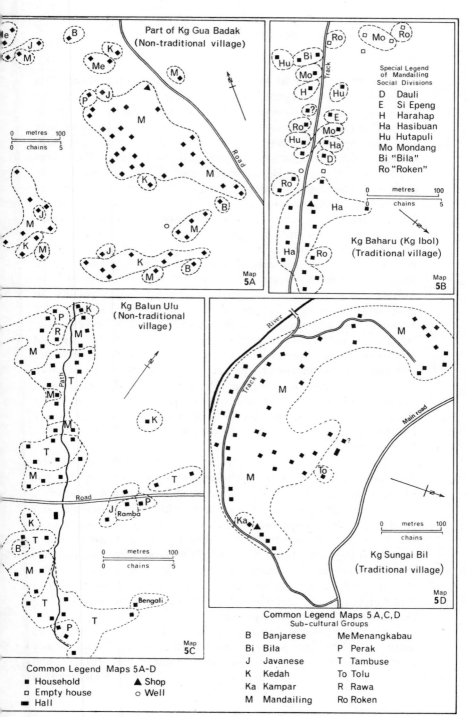

Map 5 (A, B, C, D)   Sub-cultural groups in four Mandailing villages in West Malaysia

Part of Kg Gua Badak
(Non-traditional village)

Map
5A

Kg Baharu (Kg Ibol)
(Traditional village)

Special Legend
of Mandailing
Social Divisions

D   Dauli
E   Si Epeng
H   Harahap
Ha   Hasibuan
Hu   Hutapuli
Mo   Mondang
Bi   "Bila"
Ro   "Roken"

Map
5B

Kg Balun Ulu
(Non-traditional
village)

Map
5C

Kg Sungai Bil
(Traditional village)

Map
5D

Common Legend Maps 5 A,C,D
Sub-cultural Groups

B   Banjarese   Me Menangkabau
Bi   Bila   P   Perak
J   Javanese   T   Tambuse
K   Kedah   To Tolu
Ka   Kampar   R   Rawa
M   Mandailing   Ro Roken

Common Legend Maps 5A-D

■ Household   ▲ Shop
□ Empty house   o Well
▬ Hall

be aligned along one or two main thoroughfares. In Mandailing communities in Malaya the houses are placed so that distances to be travelled are as short as possible and there is easy access to the road; there is no formal division into clan living areas because, as we have seen, clan membership is no longer socially important to most Mandailingers living in Malaysia. On walking into a village, the houses appear at first sight to be scattered about at random, but this impression is due to the unorderly planting of coconut and other trees among the houses; when a village plan is made it shows that the houses are strung out alongside well-defined lines of communication.[1] (See map 5 and plate 1.)

However, the houses of members of a sub-cultural group are never distributed at random, they are always grouped together in some way; even in villages with a large Mandailing majority, the Mandailing group is broken up into homogeneous segments. In traditional villages the segments consist of patrilineal kinsmen; for example, in Kampong Baharu (Kampong Ibol), the houses of the large dominant Hasibuan group occupy almost half the length of this linear village[2] (see map 5B), and in Kampong S. Bil there are five patrilineally related groups each with three to six households. The examination of the grouping of houses in the traditional villages suggests two principles are at work: the houses of members of the dominant group are adjacent to one another; and patrilineally related kinsmen live close together in groups of three to ten households.

The same principles apply in non-traditional and rubber-dominated villages. In some of these villages there is a large number of single units (i.e. households whose neighbours are not of the same sub-cultural group), an arrangement that reflects independent residence after marriage and sometimes a large visitor population, but in almost all non-traditional and rubber-dominated villages about half the population live in one or two large segments. Rubber-dominated villages vary more in their internal composition than wet-rice growing villages. In the former the number of households in single units varies from 4 per cent to 39 per cent, in the latter from 15 per cent to 27 per cent. (See map 5A and C.)

There is a general tendency for the number of large segments to increase as the village grows larger. Non-traditional villages usually have a bigger population than rubber-dominated villages and therefore they have more large segments. Villages with Generalized

Sumatran kin terminology, which are the largest of the non-traditional villages, have two or three large segments, but villages in which Neo-Malayan terminology is used are smaller and have only one.

If the houses of kinsmen are close together ties of kinship are strengthened by ties of neighbourship and there is no competition between kin ties and neighbour ties. On this premise a possible political interpretation of the pattern of village segmentation described above is that smaller villages are dominated by a single group, but larger villages have major factions. The point at which there is a transition from one type to the other is when there are forty to fifty households in the village.[3] This difference in internal organization has consequences for village leadership, a topic to which I shall now turn.

Headmanship

A headman is always accorded respect, but whether he is influential is another matter. In traditional Mandailing society in Sumatra the headman of the village held the title of *raja*. The office and title were inherited in the male line and therefore the perquisite of a particular patrilineal group. From the late nineteenth century until World War II Mandailing heads of villages in Sumatra performed two functions: they were head of the village according to customary law (*adat*) and therefore acted as judges in customary law cases; and they were representatives of the Dutch as lower officials in the colonial administrative hierarchy. As we have seen, the early Mandailing migrants to Malaysia willingly placed themselves under the protection of Mandailingers who obtained official rank as *Penghulu* in Malaya; in their eyes these persons performed the function of intermediary between villager and administration just as the *raja* did in Sumatra. But other migrants were trying to escape from the bonds of customary law and were looking in Malaya for entrepreneurial opportunities. This type of migrant supported his fellow Mandailingers, but was willing to accept village heads from other groups where this appeared expedient.

In two of the traditional villages the same headman has been in office for over twenty-five years (one of these headmen was recently succeeded by his son). In the other traditional villages headmen have been in office almost as long. In villages other than the traditional villages whenever the Mandailingers have a simple majority in numbers in the village they supply the headman, but the same principle applies to other Sumatran groups, so that there are villages in which there is a sizeable Mandailing minority under a non-Mandailing headman. There are also one or two villages in which there are a few Mandailing households in a village run by the traditional headman of another Sumatran group.[4] However, the principle that the headman comes from the majority group does not always apply in Perak if there is a group of Perak people in the village. The latter often supply the headman, presumably on the ground that they were the original occupants whom the Mandailingers and others joined and the headmanship therefore belongs to them.

Fig. 8. Number of years headmen and *imams* had been in office in 1973 by village type

(Data from five traditional villages, ten non-traditional villages, and six rubber-dominated villages.)

Village Type	Number of Years in Office in 1973	
	Village Headman	*Imam*
Traditional	12.8	13.3
Non-traditional	9.1	11.6
Rubber dominated	4.7	8.2

The headmanship tends to be retained by the same subcultural group, but there are signs of a change in the role which may soon result in the headmanship becoming more open to others. Prior to World War II the average length of time in office was 14.6 years; after World War II and until 1968 it was 6.8. In general, the more conservative the village, the longer the time for which a headman holds office. In 1973, the average number of years for which the then headman had held office was 4.7 in rubber-dominated villages; 9.1 in non-traditional villages, and 12.8 in traditional villages (see figure 8). Clearly, the role of headman is changing from an ascribed position with formal powers to an achieved position of prestige, and this is probably due to the government's efforts to implement its programme of social and economic development which has a better chance of success if the headman is cooperative and non-conservative. Sometimes the government has apparently enforced democracy and tried to get a headman more to its liking by insisting that elections for a new headman be held, and sometimes the villagers have responded by electing the old headman. These interesting struggles in the arena of mini-politics have been brought about as a result of the government's efforts to make the headman a minor official and a politically safe representative. Headmen with this sort of commitment to the government can get training courses and trips, rewards which would not have seemed attractive to the old-style headman whose main job was to protect the decision-making powers of the village community against encroachment from outside. While this change in the style of headmanship is taking place the attitudes of the villagers are no doubt also changing, but it seems that what matters to the Mandailingers in Malaysia is that the headman should get tangible benefits for them without becoming a "government man"; as they say of a headman in Malay, *satu kaki berjalan untuk kerajaan, satu kaki berjalan untuk orang ramai*, one foot travels for the government, one foot travels for the common people.

Imamship

Many of the early Mandailing visitors to Malaya came ostensibly to visit the religious schools in Kedah and the Mandailiners built the reputation in Malaya of being a "religious" group. This religious interest is reflected in the high proportion (79 per cent) of villages with a Mandailing component of more than 5 per cent of the total number of households that have a Mandailing *imam*.[5] Other Sumatran groups supply the *imam* in 14 per cent of these villages and the remaining 7 per cent have a Perak *imam*. The last two groups play a smaller part in religious affairs than would be justified by their numbers. This is on contrast with the role the Perak groups play in village headmanship.

In some rubber-dominated villages there are signs that the *imam*ship is becoming an open office and not the perquisite of the Mandailing group, but in most villages the office has remained with one sub-cultural group since the village was founded. The period in office up to 1968 was even longer than headmen had before World War II, with a mean of 18 years. This period is shortening most rapidly in rubber-dominated villages, and least rapidly in traditional villages, as figure 8 shows.

There does not seem to be much competition within communities to become the *imam*, although the office is a very honourable one. Most *imams* are older men who as far as one can judge are religiously inclined individuals with a sense of social responsibility. Apart from having a good character an *imam* should have had some religious training. It is probably for the last reason that Mandailingers have provided a disproportionately large number of *imams*; their greater than average wealth has made it possible for them to occasionally send a son to an Islamic college. But, as we shall see, the number of young men who get this sort of education is only about two in every hundred families (this is the pre-1963 figure and the number is now falling) so that if the community does want to have an *imam* who has had a religious education it does not have much choice.

Associations

There are associations for development, agriculture, household economy, politics, religion, women's activities, youth activities, education, and race relations (see figure 9) in villages with a Mandailing component. Some associations have a cross-village membership but most draw their membership from one village. The usual offices in an association are chairman (*pengurusi*), secretary (*setia usaha*), and treasurer (*bendahara*). There may also be a deputy chairman (*naif pengurusi*) and six or so committee members.

The interests around which associations cluster are not in themselves foreign to Mandailing culture (or the culture of any other Sumatran immigrant group); there are always women's gossip groups in Mandailing villages; there are youth groups that sometimes occupy an empty house or go to live and work in a neighbouring village to make some cash and to keep out of the way of the elders; and there are groups formed temporarily by farmers who cooperate for some economic purpose. All these groups are formed to meet the needs of a certain number of people in particular circumstances. For events that occur regularly and happen in everybody's family at some time, like births, marriages, and deaths, a work force that does what has to be done is generated by calling on appropriate kinsmen for help. When there is a wedding in a small

Fig. 9.   Types, functions, and sponsors of associations

Name	Function	Sponsor
Development		
Lembaga Kemajuan Kampong (or *Jawatan Kuasa Kemajuan Kampong)*	Village development committee	Government
Jawatan Kuasa Rayat Baik	Village development committee	Witnin village
Agriculture		
Sherikat Kilang Padi	Rice-processing co-operative	Villagers
Sherikat Getah Berkelumpok	Rubber-processing cooperative	Villagers
Persatuan Peladang	Farmers' society	Government
Gotong royong	Mutual help	Villagers
Peladang Perintis	Replaces *Persatuan Peladang* in Batu Kurau District	Government
Perkumpulan Peladang	For *gotong royong* in Kg Cholek	Villagers
Household economy		
Sharikat Kematian	Funeral club	Villagers
Sharikat Kerja Sama	Credit cooperative	Villagers
Sharikat Pinjam-meninjam	Borrowing club	Villagers
Political parties		
U.M.N.O.	Political party	Political party
P.A.S.	Political party	Political party
Religion		
Jawatan Kuasa Mesjid	Mosque committee	Villagers
Jawatan Kuasa Kuria	Mosque committee	Villagers
Women's activities		
Perkumpulan Perampuan	Women's organization	Villagers
Kaum Ibu	Mothers' organization	U.M.N.O. political party
Masakan Palawan Wanita	Women's cooking club	Villagers
Youth activities		
Persatuan Belia	Youth organization	Government
Pergerak Pemuda	Youth organization	U.M.N.O. political party
Perkumpulan Pemudapemudi	Youth organization	Villagers
Persatuan Pemuda Desa	Youth organization	Villagers
Persatuan Anak Muda Setia	Youth organization	Villagers
Education		
Lembaga Pengurus Sekolah Kebangsaan	School committee	Villagers
Persatuan Ibu-bapa	School child assistance committee (Lembah Keluang)	Villagers
Kelas Pelajaran Dewasa	Adult education class	Government
Race relations		
Jawatan Kuasa Muhipa	Race relations committee	Government

village practically everybody in the village turns out to help. If, however, there is a job that explicitly concerns everybody in the village, like 'clearing the entrance path to the village, then the work force is mobilized on the *gotong royong* principle, i.e. every family, and sometimes every person, contributes some labour, the work is divided into sections for each of which a gang is responsible, and the job is organized by the village headman.

The traditional Mandailing villages in Malaysia still use these ways of getting things done and any actions that the government requires are carried out either by groups mobilized along kinship lines or along *gotong royong* lines. People in other villages seem to be more receptive to ideas about how to organize village affairs stemming from the government but do still use the old ways of mobilizing people to get things done. However, these old ways are less effective in non-traditional and rubber-dominated villages because as we have seen the kinship systems (at least from the evidence of the kinship terminologies) do not include clearly bounded kinship groups but allow individuals to choose from among relatives those with whom they wish to maintain close relations. In short, although the interests around which some of the government-sponsored associations are organized are found in old Mandailing culture, the means by which social action is generated in relation to those interests do not accord with the formal structure of a government-sponsored association with its hierarchy of office-bearers.

The life and death of associations is commonly known in a village. Some associations lead a shadow existence; they are brought into being for a specific purpose or at the prompting of an administrative officer, have a brief active life, and then sink into the social background and become inactive. This typifies the pragmatism and flexibility that is characteristic of social processes in Malay communities.

In contrast there are associations which are continuously active because they are agencies of the government development plan and receive regular help from government officers. The village development organization (*Jawatan Kuasa Kemajuan Kampong*) is one such association which frequently involves more than one community and through which government officers attempt to sponsor regional consciousness. The women's organization may also have a cross-village membership,[6] and occasionally a mosque is shared between two villages, e.g. S. Bil and S. Darau, and the mosque maintenance committee has a cross-village membership.

Some associations are organized on a national basis with local branches, e.g. the political parties and the farmers' organization (*Persatuan Peladang*). The latter may be developed locally into an organization with a very wide range of activities covering many aspects of social welfare.[7]

In short, associations vary in origin, function, and life span. They may be used as vehicles for social change, for the exercise of power by villagers, and by government officers to increase their influence; normally they are small in scale, specialized in function, and active as need arises.

Associations with the same functions, or at least with the same name, are common throughout western Malaya, but the constellation of associations varies from village to village. There is no connection between the percentage of Mandailingers in a village and the number of associations. The number of associations increases as the total population of the village grows larger: above twenty households the number of associations is four; only very large villages, above eighty households in size, have five or six associations. Traditional, non-traditional, and rubber-dominated villages of comparable size have the same number of associations. Villages with a Generalized Sumatran kinship terminology tend to have more associations than villages with a Neo-Malayan kinship terminology but this appears to be due to their larger size. In the period 1963-68, taking all villages together, household economy associations were by far the most common, followed in order of frequency by agricultural associations, youth organizations, women's organizations, race relations committees, and political party branches of which there were two. In 1973-74 there were fifteen political party branches, making this the most common form of association, interest in agricultural associations and youth clubs was still high, and other kinds of associations were poorly represented.

Mandailing involvement in associations

In the traditional villages in 1968 there were very few associations; two youth organizations and one funeral club were the only intra-village organizations. By 1973-74 there were ten associations; four were government-sponsored agricultural associations; two were economic associations organized along kinship lines; two were political parties; and there was one youth club and one educational organization. As one headman put it, "we all help one another"; the implication was that all needs are taken care of through kinship, neighbourship, and village membership.

In 1968 the kinds of associations found in non-traditional and rubber-dominated villages were much the same. Household economy associations were the most common in both; then came associations for agriculture; women's activities; development; religion; politics; and race relations. Youth associations were common in non-traditional villages but not in rubber-dominated villages. By 1973-74 in both these types of villages political party branches were common, but household economy associations and development committees had become insignificant (see figure 10).

Fig. 10. Kind and number of associations by village type in 1973–74

Kind of Association	Village Type		
	Traditional (5 Villages)	Non-traditional (10 Villages)	Rubber-dominated (6 Villages)
Development		1	
Agriculture (government sponsored)	4	4	
Agricultural enterprise (village-sponsored)	2	2	
Household economy		1	2
Political parties	2	9	4
Women's activities		1	3
Youth activities	1	5	3
Education	1	1	

When the data from all villages for both periods are combined Mandailingers are found to be most frequently to least frequently involved as office-bearers or committee members in the order: political parties, development associations, agriculture and household economy associations (equal); women's clubs, youth clubs, educational associations, and religious organizations. Mandailingers conform with the general interest in so far as household economics, agriculture, women's activities, and religion are concerned, take a moderate interest in youth activities, but show higher than average interest in political parties and development and lower than average interest in education. In villages in which they form less than 26 per cent of the population Mandailingers hold more offices and are committee members more often than their numbers would warrant. This tendency becomes less marked as the proportion of Mandailingers in the community increases (but more rapidly in non-traditional than in rubber-dominated villages), so that in large villages Mandailingers have fewer representatives on association committees than their numbers would warrant. This might illustrate a general phenomenon, i.e. that a drive for representation on the part of minorities usually results in their being over-represented. In general, the number of offices occupied by Mandailingers is disproportionately high (except in large non-traditional villages); thus they occupy more leadership roles and this may be a result of their higher economic status.

When they first came to Malaysia, the Mandailingers were interested in religious training and seeking a fortune; the former rationalized the latter in that it encouraged individualism and economic drive. Their religious interests produced a number of *imam*s but this office has decreased in importance as formal religion has been taken over and organized by the government and at the same time has become more open to others. This accords with the loss of Mandailing interest in religion as shown by their poor membership in religious associations. On the other hand the Mandailing drive for economic success which elevated the Mandailingers to a relatively strong economic position is still evident in their interest in economic associations.

Viewing the socio-political scene as a whole, the Mandailingers were forced to share the management of village affairs in multicultural villages in Perak with Perak people who specialized in political control, and elsewhere, in all the larger villages, they were only one among three or four large factions. Wherever they found themselves lacking political influence they compensated by economic activity. This analysis is born out by the growth of associations from 1962-63 to 1973-74. In 1962-63 there were two associations in the traditional villages, a badminton club and a development committee; in 1973-74 there were, as we have seen, ten associations; six concerned with economics, two with politics, and two with social matters. In contrast, in 1962-63 there was an average of two associations per village in non-traditional and rubber-dominated villages; by 1973-74 this had grown to an average of 2.7 associations per non-traditional village, but the average had not changed in rubber-dominated villages. In these two types of village the associations that have increased in numbers most markedly are political parties; economic associations have not increased in number; and badminton and football clubs have been replaced by youth associations with wider aims. In short, in the villages in which the Mandailingers' interests are most fully expressed, i.e. the traditional villages, associations related to economic affairs are more common than they are in other villages, and it is only this kind of village-sponsored association that has increased in number in the ten years prior to 1974.

Types of schools

Universal free primary secular education for all races is a feature of modern Malaysia. Children enter school at about six to seven years of age for six years. It is said that a child can leave school before reaching class six but in fact few do. In a medium size school the numbers in a class are about forty-five; report cards are used. In secular education Malay parents have the choice of a Malay or English stream. At the secondary level, a child can be sent to an Islamic religious school, a so-called continuation school which emphasizes technical training, or to an academic middle school. Students at secondary school must pay fees, but a student from a poor family who does well at secondary school may get a subsidy of M$15-20 per month. There is also a number of long-established private schools such as the Methodist Secondary school near Ayer Tawar and the Anderson school near Ipoh. Fees at these schools are of the order of M$20 per month. There are government adult education classes for those who cannot read or write.

The Islamic religious middle schools are a special feature of Malay education and are financially supported by the government. The classes often begin in the late afternoon so that the pupils can work or attend a secular school in the morning. The curriculum always includes reading and writing Arabic, study of the Koran, Islamic behavioural codes, and Islamic canon law;[8] it may also include subjects like arithmetic or Islamic interpretations of history and world political organization. It is often necessary for a pupil to board at these schools and the cost can be M$100 per month. Some young people still go to Kedah to spend two to three months in a *pondok*.

Attendance at schools

No girls or youths from traditional villages went to secondary school until the period 1963-68 when 1.9 youths per 100 families went to secular school and 2.73 went to religious middle school. There was a small increase in the number of youths from non-traditional wet-rice growing villages who attended secondary school from the five years preceding 1962 to the 1963-68 period, but the number of girls attending such schools remained the same, so that overall the number of children attending secular secondary schools rose slightly in the later period. On the other hand there was a decrease in the numbers attending religious secondary schools. But in the rubber-dominated villages in the second period twice as many youths and almost three times as many girls attended secular high school as in the first period. On the other hand, no children attended religious middle schools. There were therefore some sharp differences between the three types of villages in 1968. In the traditional villages the only interest in secondary education was in religious education for males; in the non-traditional villages youths were sent to high school about twice as often as girls and the predominant interest was in secular education; and in the rubber-dominated villages far more children, including a proportionately larger number of girls, went to high school, but interest in high religious education was nil for youths and almost nil for girls. (See figure 11.)

Fig. 11. Secondary school attendance per 100 families

	Pre-1963				1963–68				1968–73			
	Secular		Religious		Secular		Religious		Secular		Religious	
	Male	Female	Male	Female	Male	Female	Male	Female	Male	Female	Male	Female
Traditional	0	0	0	0	1.9	0	2.73	0	10.9	9.0	3.4	3.4
Non-traditional	3.79	1.89	1.83	0	4.06	1.94	0.79	0.39	11.0		0	0.5
Rubber-dominated	5.78	3.15	0	1.56	11.5	7.19	0	0	24.8		0.5	0

Note: Separate figures for males and females for non-traditional and rubber-dominated villages are not available for 1968–73 with respect to secular education.

In the five years to 1973-74 the trends in the data for the previous periods continued in non-traditional and rubber-dominated villages. The number of children sent to secular secondary schools increased by about 100 per cent in non-traditional villages and by about 30 per cent in rubber-dominated villages;[9] the interest in religious education remained low and relatively speaking decreased. But in the traditional villages a remarkable change took place; interest in secular education blossomed, there was a tenfold increase in the number sent to secondary school, and moreover, almost half of these were girls; and at the same time the number sent to religious schools more than doubled, and again, half of these were girls.[10]

School going by Mandailingers

Do the Mandailingers in non-traditional and rubber-dependent villages send their children to secondary school and religious middle schools more often than the members of other sub-cultural groups? The answer is that they always send their male children more often than other groups, but not always their female children. Prior to 1963 in non-traditional and rubber-dominated villages the Mandailingers constituted from 55 per cent to 60 per cent of the population and provided 80 per cent of the advanced male school children at secular schools, but only 33 per cent and 50 per cent respectively of the female advanced school children at secular schools. In the 1963-68 period the relative numbers of boys sent to secular secondary school by Mandailing families increased still further in non-traditional villages, but decreased somewhat in rubber-dominated villages. In both kinds of villages the Mandailingers sent more girls to advanced secular schools and in non-traditional villages more than the average for the other sub-cultural groups. In other words, the comparative economic advantage which the Mandailingers had as landowners in the non-traditional villages has been increased by the better education which they could afford for their children, but in rubber-dominated villages their economic lead over the members of other sub-cultural groups has been and continues to be reduced, and they have not made the same educational gains. The sudden interest in education of people in the traditional villages is indicative of a breakout from cultural containment.

Merantau

The going out to seek a fortune, *merantau*, pattern spreads wider the villager's network of social ties. The villager with a relative in another village, town, or city has his social horizon widened. When the relative returns to visit, his traveller's tales provide comparative information about social and economic conditions elsewhere, and help to form opinions about regional and national issues. Life chances are reassessed by the stay-at-home, using the yardstick which the emigrant's economic success provides. Moreover, this enlargement of the social network provides the opportunity for new forms of reciprocity between members: loans to get started in business, a place to stay when visiting; and a home away from home for older children who must leave their village to go to secondary school. A family whose members have different occupations is better protected against economic recession or misfortune and its wider involvement in the Malaysian scene can lead to a greater sense of identity with Malaysia and commitment to Malaysia as a nation. *Merantau* is therefore important to our theme; I shall call it trial emigration.

There are considerable differences in the pattern of trial emigration and hence its sociological effects from one village type to another and from one village to another. Data are available for the five years prior to 1962, for 1963-68, and for 1968-73. The mean number of men per 100 families moving out from traditional villages has been relatively low but slowly rising (9, 10, and 11 for the three periods respectively); for non-traditional villages the figures are 11, 14, and 16 respectively, and for rubber-dominated villages 16, 15, and 17 (see figure 12). In other words, trial emigration of youths from traditional villages is low and constant, there was a sharp rise in emigration from non-traditional villages from the first to the second period and then a falling off, and emigration of youths from rubber-dominated villages has been and still is relatively high and constant.

Fig. 12. Trial emigration per 100 families by village type and sex

	Pre-1963		1963–68		1968–73	
	Male	Female	Male	Female	Male	Female
Traditional villages	9	–	10	–	11	7
Non-traditional villages	11	–	16	–	14	5
Rubber-dominated villages	16	–	15	–	17	9

A real surprise is the sudden appearance in all three types of villages of trial emigration by young women.

The traditional villages in Negeri Sembilan which are surrounded by a culturally different milieu had no trial emigration until 1968[11] but the rate from traditional villages elsewhere was at about the same level as in nearby non-traditional wet-rice growing villages. It appears that for trial emigration to take place at all there must be generally similar social conditions in the surrounding region into which the emigrant can move or the emigrant must be able to move into a cultural pocket to which his or her existing social network stretches.

The rise in trial emigration from non-traditional villages in the 1963-68 period could be due to the development of an adequate social network but the subsequent fall-off suggests that changes in local economic conditions have an important effect. The very considerable range of variation (from 4 to 35) in the rate per 100 families shows that conditions vary widely from village to village. Some of the figures at the extremes of the range are easy to account for. Parit-parit 15-18B, for example, which until about 1970 had a low rate of trial emigration, is sited on a development scheme and there were opportunities for acquiring land locally but about 1970 the supply of land ceased and emigration started; and the very high rate of Kg Lasah in the pre-1963 period was apparently due to a decision by a group of related youths to join the army together. There is some negative correlation in non-traditional villages between village size and rate of trial emigration and this suggests that in the larger villages economic and social differentiation provided space for social movement until about 1968, but since then a much more important factor has been the land development schemes and local industries whose development has been aided under the Second Malaysia Plan and which have provided employment and so slowed down trial emigration. At Kg Balun twenty men and women earn wages (*makan gaji*) as labourers with the Department of Public Works, in minor industries in Selim River, or in various jobs with the timber-getting industry; at S. Chinchin about thirty men and women work as labourers in Kuala Lumpur and fifty women work in a nearby factory; at S. Sekiah about forty people have daily work in various jobs and twenty have permanent work in a nearby government office; and at Pekan Ulu Langat nearly one hundred men and women have daily work in Kajang or on government projects. Associated with these opportunities for local employment is another factor—the loss of rice fields. At Balun the wet-rice fields have not been in use since 1968 owing to impairment of the irrigation scheme; at S. Chinchin a water shortage started in 1970 and the wet-rice fields have not been used since; of the 32 hectares of wet-rice fields at S. Sekiah only 12 were in use in 1973[12]; and at Lasah where it is said there were formerly 81 hectares of wet-rice land only 20 are now being worked. The men and women who formerly worked these fields must either get jobs locally or emigrate.

In the non-traditional villages the Mandailingers form a disproportionately large part of the total number of emigrants. Although comprising 39 per cent of the population in the pre-1963 period they formed 75 per cent of the migrants; this was reduced to 58 per cent in the period 1963-68 and has since probably been reduced further.

In rubber-dominated villages there is also a wide range of variation in the rate of *merantau* per 100 families, but the correlation with size, though negative, is low. This suggests that the opportunities for youth within the rubber-dominated villages are less than they are in the larger non-traditional villages and this is understandable when one considers that rubber requires a relatively long growing period before it gives a yield. Moreover, many of the rubber-dependent villages are sited in areas that are not suitable for development projects; in Kinta, for example, there is no timber getting and space for agricultural expansion is very limited. Local employment is available on only a limited scale; for example, at Kg Mesjid (Kg Banir) one woman and four men work at the local lime works, at Kg Mesjid (Timoh Setesen) four people work locally for wages, and at Pusing some men and women commute to Ipoh to work for wages. In these villages the Mandailingers have little or no more land than the members of other sub-cultural groups, the same economic constrictions apply to all and we find that the proportion of Mandailingers in the total population (51 per cent) is close to the proportion of Mandailingers among the emigrants (54 per cent).

In the pre-1963 period the range of occupations to which emigrants moved was small. In the non-traditional villages 15 per cent became rubber tappers or engaged in some other rural occupation, 81 per cent joined the army or police, and only 4 per cent went to factory or other city jobs. In the 1963-68 period however, the number going into rural occupations had fallen to 8 per cent, and the number going into the army or police to 45 per cent; 23 per cent became teachers or clerks, 25 per cent went to factory or city jobs (a sixfold increase), and 3 per cent went to development projects. In the rubber-dominated villages the range of occupations to which emigrants went was similar, but even fewer (2 per cent) took up rural occupations and none went to development projects. Mandailing emigrants from both non-traditional and rubber-dominated villages preferred rubber tapping and city jobs to the other occupations. In short, in non-traditional villages the Mandailingers formed a disproportionate amount of the total emigrant population; and in both non-traditional and rubber-dominated villages they favoured cash-yielding occupations rather than establishment positions in the army, police, or teaching service. The Mandailing interest in economic affairs is expressed once again, and this point is underlined by the fact that of the first emigrants from the traditional villages the largest proportion went to factory or city jobs in which they had opportunities for earning money.

In the 1968-73 period the pattern of trial emigration changed quite markedly in all three types of villages: women became a significant part of the emigrant stream and by 1974 more than half the total number of emigrants were women; of the trial emigrants from traditional villages, one third entered the army or police which thus absorbed a large proportion of the male emigrants, one fifth went to a factory or labouring job in the city, and as a result of the blossoming of interest in secular education, the largest proportion (37 per cent) became teachers or clerks (see figure 13).

Fig. 13. Occupations of trial emigrants in the 1968–73 period by village type (Expressed as percentages of all trial emigrants from each village type.)

	Traditional Villages	Non-traditional Villages	Rubber-dependent Villages
Rural occupation (e.g. rubber tapping, odd jobs)	–	2	1
Army or police	33	30	11
Teachers or clerks	37	26	72
Factory or labouring in the city	21	30	10
Nurse	3	5	3
Other professions	6	7	3

Trial emigrants from the non-traditional villages entered a wider variety of occupations than previously, about equal numbers entered the army or police, became teachers or clerks, or went to factory or labouring jobs in the city, and the number seeking other rural occupations became insignificant. In the rubber-dependent villages the pay-off from the longer interest in secular education (especially for girls) is shown in the very high proportion of trial emigrants (72 per cent) who became teachers or clerks; only one-fifth of all emigrants entered the army or police or took factory or labouring jobs in the city. The wishes of trial emigrants of the future is probably indicated by the choice of occupation that the trial emigrants from the rubber-dependent villages have made; even in the traditional villages, the number entering the army or police, which formerly absorbed up to 80 per cent of rural emigrants, is exceeded by the number who become teachers or clerks. This is a significant change in the interests of the Mandailingers; they are no longer looking for jobs that produce cash only, they are looking for jobs that also give status.

Visiting Sumatra

Mandailingers in Sumatra often reaffirm their family ties by a visit to their natal village at *Hari Raya*, the period of festivities following the end of the fasting month of Rhamadan, and they make visits at other times in order to pay their respects to parents or to settle matters of family business. Such visits have also been made by Mandailing emigrants in Malaya in spite of the relatively great cost.

But the number per village of those whose visits to Sumatra are remembered is rather small—usually two or three.[13] From the traditional village of Kerangai an exodus of a part of the population back to Sumatra took place in 1922, fifteen years after the village was founded. Those who went were said to have been "called back" by their relatives in Sumatra, an indication of the strength of the ties between emigrants and their natal village. Yet mass visiting to Sumatra has never occurred and therefore whose who have made the visit are socially significant people. Most of the visitors are men and 25 per cent of them in fact are at present in important positions in their village like village headman or religious judge.

In several villages it was commented that making visits to

Sumatra was quite common before World War II, and sometimes village members who made regular trips were mentioned. The dates on which individuals were said to have visited Sumatra support this statement but they also show that most of the trips were made before 1930.

Most of the visitors made their visit to Sumatra between eleven and thirty years after their village in Malaya was founded, but some visitors went forty to sixty years after their village was founded. The idea of visiting persisted although the number of visits was reduced right through the economic recession of the 1930s, World War II, the Emergency period, and the period of Indonesian Confrontation of Malaysia. Only since about 1965 have the military-political situation and the financial standing of the Mandailingers in Malaya made visits possible and the number of visits is probably now increasing. The available data show that there is no difference in the number of visitors from traditional, non-traditional and rubber-dominated villages.

The date of a visit is well remembered and like the pilgrimage to Mecca an important mark in a man's life. Most visitors travel alone, but some have a male companion and a few take their wives. The visit has the air of a pilgrimage about it, of paying respect to one's forebears, following the pattern of the Mandailingers in Sumatra, but the comments of the visitors on their return about the rule of custom, political developments, and economic progress show that the framework of observation is that of a person on *merantau*. Most visitors see the situation in Sumatra as having changed little since pre-World War II days, but many people still want to visit. In 1968 a new cross-Straits boat service from Malacca to Dumai was instituted and news of this was going round the villages.

In the period 1968-73 forty-four men, sixteen women, and a few children from twenty-four villages visited Sumatra; there were only two villages from which visitors did not go. Sixty-six per cent of the visitors went by air from Penang to Medan, and the rest by ship, most of them from Penang to Belawan and a few from Malacca to Dumai or Singapore to Pakan Baru.[14] The visitors from the traditional villages showed a preference for travel by sea, and stayed in Sumatra for an average of nine weeks, while the visitors from non-traditional and rubber-dependent villages preferred air travel and stayed for an average of three weeks. Eighty per cent of the visitors from the non-traditional and rubber-dependent villages were

Mandailingers and the rest were members of other sub-cultural groups originating from Sumatra (Menangkabau, Tambuse, Acheh, and Kampar). In both types of villages there were proportionately slightly more visitors from the Mandailing part of the population than from the other Sumatran groups, but it is certainly evident that members of other sub-cultural groups as well as the Mandailingers maintain their ties with their villages of origin in Sumatra. Moreover these ties are being made firmer by return visits from Sumatra to Malaysia; since 1971 members of at least eight Mandailing communities in Malaysia have been visited by relatives from Sumatra.[15]

The Mandailing image

In any society people in different positions have different views of the same phenomenon.[16] In Malaysia higher and lower officials, teachers and villagers have different images of the Mandailingers in Malaysia.

The Mandailingers of the traditional villages in Negeri Sembilan have a clear-cut identity. The higher officials there tend to inherit a stereotyped view of them as very hard-working people who are loyal to their local group leader whom they support strongly—"he can get more out of them than we can"; as people who like to keep to and marry among themselves; and whose communal feeling is especially evident at wedding ceremonies and funerals. They are said to be related to Mandailingers in Selangor who pay them visits. In Selangor and Perak similarly well-educated higher officials know of the Mandailinger's role in nineteenth century Malaysian history but their views of the contemporary Mandailingers are often in phantasy form. It is said, for example, that their women are famous for their beauty, but that they are wicked. A common view, and a more nearly correct one, is that Mandailingers always look for other Mandailingers. It is also said that formerly they did not like to marry with Perak people.

There are lower officials including *Penghulu* who do not know the difference between one Sumatran cultural group and another and some who probably rightly regard such differences as irrelevant to their job. But most *Penghulu* who can recognize the Mandailingers as a culturally distinct group make earthy judgments about them based on practical experience. In Negeri Sembilan the

Mandailingers are said to be careful, hard working, religious, honest, and very straightforward. Reference is made to their interest in economics by describing how their women sell vegetables. In the Kajang District they are said to be very mean, very law abiding, and, as pioneers, owners of much land. They are also described as disputatious. They command respect, it is said, among other people of Indonesian origin because they save money and help their children.

In Perak they are also described as hard working and industrious, but it is believed that they can work magic or use *santau* which when put in food makes people mad or sick. In the Ayer Tawar area they are said to follow a leader much better than other Malays; they are described as well organized, with their own scholarship fund, mosque building fund, religious school fund, and burial cooperative. They are said to be in English idiom "smart chaps".

A few teachers who can find their way through the complexities of Malaysian group origins say that the Mandailingers were formerly the same as Bataks; that when in Sumatra they became Muslims and so "raised their standards". Their customary law (*adat*) changed, especially in relation to marriage, death, and childbirth. A more pejorative view is the description of the Mandailingers as "Bataks disguised as Muslims".[17]

Non-Mandailing villagers make jokes about the stinginess of the Mandailingers: "If I ask my mother for money and she won't give it, I say 'just like a Mandailinger'." A spokesman for a Kualo group commenting on the Mandailingers gave what is probably a representative view: "They look out for themselves; they are not afraid of people; the Mandailingers and the Chinese are much the same; they are clever, they will not sell at a loss; they are also clever at using words. The Bila people try to make possessions from working in gardens, not from trading; the Mandailingers try to get possessions but they are willing to sell and to trade when they can. The Mandailingers do not like neighbours to come to their house, they think it will cost something; not so the Bila and the Kualo."

From their side the Mandailingers in Perak describe the indigenous Perak Malays as "really from Sakai[18], but one cannot say so; formerly they had no Islam". In Negeri Sembilan they call the local matrilineal people among whom they live "Malays".

Some Mandailingers in the rubber-dominated villages of Perak attempt to hide their origins. At Chemor (established 1905) I was told by a community leader that there were really no "Mandailingers" there because they were all born in Malaya and so were their fathers (the latter statement is untrue). The same argument was used at Tanjong Rambutan (established 1907), all except one were born in Malaya it was said. At Changkat (established 1875) I was told that there was now no difference between Mandailing, Tolu, and Perak. The customary law (*adat*) which the Mandailingers had brought with them had been renewed and called *adat Melayu*, customary law of Malaya. If you ask any "Perak" man where he comes from, my informant added, eventually it will turn out that he had origins in Sumatra.

"Passing" is used by people of Mandailing origin when convenient. In one village I was told the majority of people do not know the difference between one Sumatran and another. Only Sumatrans know what a Mandailing is although other people can recognize a Sumatran. In this village the people did not know that the *imam* was a Mandailinger since he posed as a member of the dominant Sumatran group in the community. In one small trading community a number of Mandailingers said that they were Malaysians and did not regard themselves as belonging to any other group. Regional identity is sometimes used to obscure descent. If you say a person is *orang Kelang* (a Kelang man) it was pointed out you do not know what his descent is. Similarly a person from Kajang can be described as *orang Selangor* (a Selangor man).

These circumlocutions are sometimes used with characteristic Malay politeness to avoid embarrassment to individuals, but they are also more commonly heard in the presence of officials in order to avoid statements contrary to government policy or propaganda. Thus an important religious leader in the Kajang District said in the presence of the *Penghulu* that although people in the area originally came from different parts of Sumatra they were now one, although the marriage pattern (of which the religious leader was aware since he registered the marriages) and the form of local organization demonstrated the viability of localized sub-cultural groups.

In summary the imagery of Malaysian citizenship is weakly established in the minds of the villagers. The Mandailingers are described in similar terms wherever their presence is recognized, regional variations being explicable in terms of their local economic role. In the lives of the villagers kinship determines their identity, but for the upwardly mobile "passing" can have its uses; during the period of Indonesian resurgence under Sukarno it was popular to be a Sumatran, but during Confrontation it was safer to be a Malaysian. Since then the Malaysian government has tempted members of all Malay sub-cultural groups to identify themselves as *bumiputra*, sons of the land, the natural inheritors of the Malay tradition and rights. The effect of this move on the identity of the Mandailingers will be taken up in the next chapter.

Malayanization: past and future

Introduction

So far we have described separately three different but related matters: the movement of Mandailingers from Sumatra to Malaysia; internal changes within the Mandailing communities; and the participation by members of those communities in the Malaysian polity. In this chapter we shall try to demonstrate the relationships of these matters by putting their elements into a single methodological framework, in which are distinguished explanatory variables, extraneous controlled variables, and extraneous uncontrolled variables.[1] The explanatory variables include the variables which are to be explained (also often called dependent variables) and the variables with which they are related (independent variables); with respect to these variables all other variables are extraneous. The extraneous controlled variables are those variables outside the system to be explained whose effect is known (or thought to be known); the extraneous uncontrolled variables are variables which are assumed to be randomized errors. The effects of some uncontrolled extraneous variables may be confounded with those of explanatory variables.

The first section of this chapter deals with the conditions for Malayanization. The first of these conditions is, of course, migration to Malaysia and in this section this is the dependent variable. The extraneous controlled variables are world trade and political relations and the explanatory variables are conditions in Sumatra and internal conditions in Malaysia. From the relationship between these two is derived an hypothesis of migration in terms of comparative advantage. The final part of this section deals with the policies of the British period and Malaysia period which are regarded as uncontrolled variables and treated as randomized errors.

In the second section the explanatory model is changed in order to describe various processes of Malayanization. These processes are treated as the result of the operation of bundles of explanatory variables acting together. The dependent variables are various elements of Mandailing culture. This section finishes with a discussion of a terminal situation in Malayanization, i.e. assimilation.

In the third section of the chapter the key question of identity is taken up and an attempt is made to elucidate the variables involved in order to demonstrate an alternative to assimilation, i.e. the use of more than one identity.

The final section of the chapter looks at the way in which governments in Malaysia have attempted to effect Malayanization by conscious planning, or, in terms of our explanatory model, how governments have attempted to move the administrative context from the category of an uncontrolled variable treated as random error to the category of explanatory variable. Special attention is given to the new processes of Malayanization generated by the government development plans.

Conditions for Malayanization

The flow of migrants: external conditions

The great majority of Mandailing communities in Malaysia were first founded in the period between 1899 and 1916. Why were migrants moving to Malaysia at this time and why did they not come at other times? The demands of world trade stimulated the development of the tin industry in Malaysia in the late nineteenth century but the technological skills of the Malays were inadequate for large-scale exploitation, an economic activity which was dominated by the Chinese and later by the Europeans. But the Malay smallholder's skill could meet the demand for rubber and this demand grew precisely at the time when the Mandailingers began to stream to Malaysia to form the Mandailing communities that we can identify today. However, if there was a connection between these two phenomena it was only a temporary and perhaps a coincidental one, because after World War I the demand for rubber continued to increase yet the stream of Mandailing pioneer migrants ceased.[2] The effect of the decline in world trade in the late 1920s and early 1930s on the migration stream is not clear; certainly there was no large-scale movement of migrants from Sumatra to Malaysia but one Mandailing community did move back to Sumatra and there was some internal movement within Selangor and Perak. Another way to look at the effects of world trade on migration is to see whether world trade conditions created a better economic climate in Sumatra. The evidence is that the economic recession of the thirties had a fairly severe effect on those communities in Sumatra which had come to depend on rubber, but no doubt these conditions affected similar communities in Malaya in the same way. In summary the evidence for the effect of world trade conditions on the migration stream is rather slight and we can put this variable in the extraneous controlled category.

The effect of international relations in the area on the migrant stream is clear cut because they created a barrier to movement across the Straits of Malacca, and as the times at which this happens are known we can regard this effect as an extraneous controlled variable. We have to distinguish between permanent and casual movement. Apparently until World War II there was no barrier to either, but after World War II national identity became a key factor, and there was a period from about 1950 to 1955 when the new nation of Indonesia might have seemed a more attractive political entity in which to live. Temporary visiting started up again, but Confrontation stopped it. When Confrontation ended visiting began again. I think we must see temporary visiting as a means of keeping open the migration channel—both ways!

The flow of migrants: internal conditions

Internal economic conditions in countries with a relatively small number of major export products are likely to reflect the vagaries of world trade but the effects of rise and fall in demand differ from country to country because each has its own economic and social policies. The Dutch attempted to control rubber production in the 1930s in Sumatra by a permit-to-grow system which may have limited rubber production but also resulted in a flourishing market in permits, and may have brought about some redistribution of land holdings. On the whole the Mandailing homeland was probably a slightly better place to live than Malaya in the depression years because crop diversity was greater there. But this was not always so. The Dutch were slow to introduce rubber into central Sumatran areas like Mandailing where coffee grew well and the introduction of another major export crop would have upset established modes of production and marketing, and caused some internal movement of population because rubber occupies a different ecological niche from coffee. In Malaya on the other hand there was a rubber boom prior to World War I. Boom conditions subsided but the returns from rubber growing have always remained relatively higher in Malaya because of the research effort put into the development of high-yielding varieties from the plantations, especially since World War II. Consequently the smallholder's purchasing power in cash has remained fairly steady in spite of falling rubber prices. Not so in Sumatra where the lack of research, the continued use of old gardens, and the lack of replanting have led to a deterioration of income from rubber.

It is one thing to have the know-how and the will to grow rubber, another to have the land to grow it on and the means of subsistence while the crop is maturing. Land for rubber growing was probably not in short supply prior to World War I in Mandailing, Sumatra, but wet-rice land had almost reached its limits of growth using contemporary Mandailing techniques by the turn of the century. In addition the perception of the Mandailinger of that period was that the basis of subsistence, i.e. wet rice, deserved most of his agricultural effort, rubber and coffee were side-lines which produced some cash. From this point of view Malaya was very attractive. Wet-rice land was readily available to "Malays" and there was rubber land nearby to go with it. In short the key factor in promoting migration (and therefore our major explanatory variable) was the pressure on wet-rice land in Mandailing and the availability of wet-rice land in Malaya, an analysis which accords with the reported reasons given by members of contemporary Mandailing communities in Malaysia for the migration of the founding fathers.

But once the search for land was successful what next? Malaya was a terminus in the search for land, yet even under the conditions of relative land scarcity which began to develop prior to World War I in the western states and which resulted in the enclosure of the Malay reservations, the Mandailing migrants were not prepared to move across the central divide to the eastern part of Malaya.[3] Nor did they do so when grossly disturbed by tin-mining operations in Selangor and Perak. They preferred to change their economic style and become dependent solely on rubber. A new factor, educational opportunity, may have entered the picture at this point. The Man-dailingers appreciated the religious educational opportunities in Kedah where they made use of the *pondok* system although they rarely settled, and they may have appreciated also the secular educa-tion that was available in Malaya but not in Sumatra. By remaining in the more developed parts of western Malaya they could avail themselves of these facilities and still remain in touch with their Sumatran homeland only a short journey away across the Straits of Malacca. To summarize, given the over-riding importance to the prospective settler of getting access to wet-rice land there was a dif-ference from the Mandailing point of view in the ecology and social organization of Kedah, Perak and Selangor, and Negeri Sembilan. The first was an ecologically replete region, culturally well developed and held together by an administrative system stemming from the state's Hindu origins, for temporary migrants the luxury of a religious education was available at a price, although this was not the place for landless fortune hunters; Perak and Selangor, on the other hand, were in a state of political and economic flux, from time to time fortunes could be made in war, in mining, in trading and by the acquisition of land, but in the middle and late parts of the nineteenth century the structure of the economic-political system which dominates contemporary West Malaysia was present in nas-cent form—the indigenous Malay political leaders held the reins of power but they lacked the economic expertise and labour force to ex-ploit the resources of their estates. Migrants were welcome.

The economic situation in Negeri Sembilan was similar but not the socio-political organization; instead of the empty shells of mini-empires, there was a strong social fabric at the grass roots level. Migrants could become part of the pattern or search for an unoc-cupied and economically inferior ecological niche.

A hypothesis of comparative advantage

A migrant had several decisions to make of which the two most important were to try his luck abroad and the decision to stay there. These two decisions were formulated differently in custom. The first constituted *merantau*, wandering about the economic scene in search of a "fortune", the second *pindah*, removal from his village of origin to another place.[4] Both decisions were dependent on the free flow of information from Malaya to Sumatra and vice versa; at one time people moved to "Haji Dollah's place" where it was known that work was available. A married man had to think in longer terms of how he would establish himself. Persons who pioneered new sites appear to have been rapidly joined by others and these people formed a migrant group, which we can conveniently use as a sociological unit. The possibility of forming or joining such a unit must have been one of the important factors which a potential migrant considered when weighing the comparative advantages of residence in one place or another. The other most important factor of course was the availability of wet-rice fields. The first-formed migrant group was a dynamic group in the sense that it was in interaction with its immediate economic and social context and with the particular cultural stream from which it was generated. It was usually composed of kinsmen, not always from the same village but from the same area, who shared a common *adat*. Later the group was joined by others and developed its own village culture and internal organization and a means for regulating its external relations. During the process of growth there was probably a turnover in the population of the group.[5] While it was possible to travel across the Straits of Malacca, this turnover probably included persons who came from and went to Sumatra; when the Straits were closed the intake and outflow was from and to other communities in Malaysia. The necessary conditions for making a move were the free flow of information about the conditions of life in different places and the freedom of action of the potential migrant. The sufficient condition for migration was that he should see comparative advantage in making the move.

Malayanization interpreted: the British period

Prior to World War II there was little pressure on the Mandailingers in Malaya to Malayanize. They were treated by the administration as "Malays" along with the culturally very different Javanese and Banjarese; access to land and to education was as open to them in the area in which they lived as it was to the indigenous Malays; socially they were classified as "foreign Malays". There was a free flow of information about the conditions of life in Malaysia and Sumatra through the constant intervisiting to and fro across the Straits. In the twenty years before World War I the comparative advantage as far as access to wet-rice land was concerned lay with Malaysia and this was the period of founding and develop- ment of new Mandailing communities there. But after that there was little to choose between Malaya and Sumatra and individuals seeking their fortune moved to and fro across the Straits. Gradually however in the established communities many persons came to have an economic stake in Malaya which they could not easily give up. In those communities which were displaced and re-adapted themselves to living alongside other culture groups there were internal cultural changes which led to a new sense of identity as persons living in a particular part of Malaya—they became part of a social net which spread through Malaya as intermarriage with local Mandailingers took place and across the Straits through kinship ties to particular villages.

While these internal changes were taking place in village culture, the external political, administrative, and economic scene was also evolving, in each state and in Malaya as a whole. Religion was the vehicle through which new political ideas entered Malaya at the beginning of this century, though not everyone took up the new ideas; a difference grew between *kaum tua* and *kaum muda*, the former supporting traditional rule, the latter the introduction of democracy along Western lines and some curtailment of the power of the sultans. In 1925 there were twenty-seven Malay students at Al-Azhar University in Cairo with advanced political ideas and "strange" notions of union with Indonesia (Soenarno 1960, p.10).[6] Secular education also brought about a change in political consciousness, the Malay stream fostering notions of pan-Malayan unity and the English stream ideas of economic and national development. Thus there were present in the early 1930s all the ideas which crystallized in political parties formed just before or after World War II, and which are, in fact, still present in contemporary Malaysia. "By 1905", says Soenarno (p.3), "the need for validating one's position by education had been realised" and this led as a matter of course to a role in administration,[7] while, at the same time, the Malays adandoned trading and craftsmanship.[8] How far these ideas of learning, progress, and development penetrated into Mandailing communities in West Malaysia is an open question; certainly it is likely that some of the wealthier villagers contributed to Malay enlightenment by providing an education for their sons,[9] and so linked the cultural stream of the village-farmer and that of the teacher-intellectual.

Malayanization interpreted: the Malaysia period

The Japanese helped the idea of nationhood to emerge when they upset the established balance of power and gave back to the traditional Malayan elite a new consciousness of rulership. This level of political action was far above the heads of the migrant groups for whom the key variables were local security and the power of their economic efforts to return them a living. The Malaysian leaders hoped through education to bring about a new consciousness of identity.[10] But from the villagers' point of view the rationalization of the educational system made little difference to their view of the world. The possibility of getting a secular education for one's children was one of the comparative advantages which Malaya had had over Sumatra in the period between the World Wars; but the notion that access to higher education was available only to those of high status who could exert political pressure was also present. Moreover Indonesia made educational history in the region in the 1950s by bringing primary education to every villager and making secondary education available to the child of any parent who could pay. The comparative advantage of Malaya in this field vanished.[11] Far more important as stimuli were the enforced shifts of locale, the drama of the Emergency period, and the opportunity which Confrontation offered for presentation of the idea of Malaysia as a nation.

Confrontation provided a testing time for the allegiance and identity of Sumatran immigrants in Malaysia. According to Indonesian propaganda the political power of the Malays was nominal and the Chinese represented a menace to the Malays inside their own country (Pluvier 1965). In 1963 the Indonesian ambassador to Malaysia was openly visiting Malays' and Indonesians' homes in Malaya "spreading anti-Chinese propaganda". The Malays he said could get "safety within the realms of the Malay fold"; similar ideas were spread through the Malay left-wing parties and in September 1963 the Republic of Malays was instituted by the *Kesatuan Melayu Muda* (The Young Malay Party) in Indonesia (Wan Kalthom 1970). The burning of the effigy of Tungku Abdul Rahman in Jakarta in May 1963 was interpreted by most Malays as an insult to their leaders and was helpful in bringing about a turn around in Malay attitudes led by U.M.N.O, the main Malay political party of which Tungku Abdul Rahman was leader. The Sultan of Johore said that he knew of the presence of many Malays of Indonesian origin in his state, that he would do his utmost to oppose subversion, and that he saw the state's people as supporting the government through their voting for U.M.N.O. (Wan Kalthom 1970). The government took the opportunity to arrest some of its political opponents who were known to have pro-Indonesian sympathies.[12] When Confrontation was officially terminated by the signing of a treaty on 12 August 1966, the representatives from both Indonesia and Malaysia spoke of the people on the two sides of the Straits of Malacca as people of one race, an attitude that did not encourage the idea of Malaysia but probably reflected what was in the minds of the Mandailingers in Malaysia.

Malaysia[13] came into existence on 31 August 1963 and in its development planning the Malaysian government got very rapidly to the source of possible rural unrest, i.e. land shortage in a period of rapid population expansion. This contrasts with the situation in Upper Mandailing where the author's observations show that the population increased by an average of 25 per cent from 1956 to 1971 and the available wet-rice fields scarcely at all. The Federal Land Development Authority (F.L.D.A.) schemes recreated once more the pre-World War I situation of land availability for the venturesome pioneer. But the land, though cheap in monetary terms, could be had only if some traditional freedoms were sacrificed. I shall return to this point.

The efforts of the Malaysian government to develop the country undoubtedly had an effect on the pace of Malayanization. But before dealing with this topic I shall have a look at the processes of Malayanization that have emerged so far. The explanatory variables have been identified, they are access to land, access to education, maintenance of the cultural integrity of the community, and identification with a cultural stream; the dependent variables are elements of Mandailing culture. I shall now look at the ways in which a migrant group, having found its own cultural niche and developed its own ecosystem, is changed by internal strain arising from growth or pressure of external events; new variables are not introduced; what we do is to show how in the course of time accidents of place and contact induce strain in the culture of the migrant group, a poorness of fit of the cultural elements which brings about social and cultural change.

Processes of Malayanization

The migrant groups of Mandailingers in Malaysia are composed of social fragments which broke off from their parent bodies in Sumatra and were re-formed into viable communities in Malaysia. Each developed its peculiar features in Malaysia as the ingredients with which it started reacted to the particular economic circumstances and social contacts that it experienced.[14] I shall now deal with some of the processes which affected the course of internal culture change.

Isolation

There is no discernible relationship between date of founding and physical isolation. No doubt all Mandailing communities when they were founded were somewhat more isolated than they are today, but in contemporary Malaysia some of the villages with a high percentage of Mandailing families are in relatively densely populated parts of West Malaysia, e.g. Kampong Mesjid (Kampong Banir) (86.6 per cent), Kampong Mesjid (Timoh Setesen) (79.9 per cent), Batu 4 (Selim river) (86.9 per cent), and Sungai Bil (91.2 per cent). The last two are traditionally oriented villages in which the headman has been in office for many years,[15] the first two are rubber-dominated villages. The three other villages with a high proportion of Mandailingers (nearly 100 per cent) are Kerangai, Kampong Bahru (K. Ibol), and Kampong Tambah Tin, all which are in Negeri Sembilan. Langkap (founded 1914) is the mother village of the three and is situated in a physically isolated high site which was not used for wet-rice cultivation by the surrounding population. The isolation is such that the village was abandoned on orders from the administration during the Emergency. This stimulated the founding of Kampong Baharu (Kampong Ibol) in 1951, but some of the members of this village are moving back to Langkap, owing to the high rents charged for the hire of the wet-rice fields they are at present using. Kerangai was founded in 1926 and its offshoot Kampong Tambah Tin in 1955. The latter is occupied by younger families and is close to a market town.

This history of settlement, although having some unique features, illustrates some features which must have characterized early Mandailing migration and settlement: the first chosen site was physically isolated, but wet-rice land was available; the settlers avoided hiring wet-rice fields and tried to get land of their own; and when the parent settlement outgrew its ecological base or there were internal dissensions (the two may of course be closely related) an off-shoot settlement was founded. Finally it shows that in contemporary Malaysia younger people are attracted by an urbanized milieu, and will accept inferior conditions in order to live there.

The unique feature about this capsule settlement history is the sharp difference between Mandailing culture and the culture of the surrounding people. There has been no intermarriage between the Mandailingers and the "Malays" of Negeri Sembilan. Yet this cultural difference is surely one of degree, not of kind. In twenty-one of the remaining twenty-nine settlements in which there is a Mandailing component there are also indigenous, i.e. Perak and Selangor, Malays. In these settlements only four marriages of Mandailing men to Perak women and four marriages of Mandailing women to Perak men have been recorded from 1963 to 1968. All the marriages were with persons from outside each of the five villages concerned. In other words although the cultural difference between Mandailinger and Perak Malay is less sharp than the cultural difference between Mandailinger and Negeri Sembilan Malay, the rate of marriage between Mandailingers and Perak Malays still remains low, and the marriages are of a kind which does little damage to the cultural integrity of the Mandailing community.

In summary, physical isolation has not been an important explanatory variable in relation to culture change in the Mandailing communities. Those youths who wanted a more exciting life than their natal village could offer found it temporarily by following the *merantau*, fortune seeking, pattern. In recent times however there are signs that some younger people are wanting to try out a different life style and they express this by moving to a new site. In the Ulu Langat Valley several Indonesian sub-cultures are represented, but even though the settlements are long established and there has been some intermarriage between their members the limits of areas occupied by different sub-culture groups are recognizable. The villages display ribbon development along roads and appear to be contiguous, although in fact the administrative boundaries are well known, but the latter do not coincide with the cultural boundaries: there are groups of Mandailing houses, Menangkabau houses, Rawa houses, and houses of other sub-cultural groups. This kind of distribution we have already shown (chapter 6) is characteristically found inside villages in which more than one cultural group is represented. The physical layout reflects the social isolation from which a sense of identity is generated.

Segmentation

Segmentation is the division of a community into two or three parts which may themselves form new communities. Two forms of segmentation were illustrated in the history of the Langkap community. The first was the voluntary segmentation which took place in 1926 when Kerangai was formed in the traditional Mandailing manner by the movement of a member of a *raja* family with a group of followers. The second was the induced segmentation which took place when Langkap had to be abandoned during the Emergency period; some members of the community went to Kerangai and others formed the new community of Kampong Baharu (New Village) (Kampong Ibol). Voluntary segmentation in the early stages of community growth is not often found in the history of Mandailing communities in West Malaysia. Quarrels among early settlers are not mentioned, in fact some communities are said to have been founded jointly by two or three people. Voluntary segmentation usually takes place when the community outgrows its resources—it cannot offer leadership roles to ambitious men, or, more usually, land scarcity develops owing to the growth of the population.

Induced segmentation is brought about by administrative action. From the 1930s onwards this took the form in Perak and Selangor of allowing tin-mining operations to take precedence over any other form of land use, thus forcing the people off their wet-rice fields, and in the Emergency period moving communities for security reasons. The Mandailingers who were forced to move during the Emergency to form Kampong Baharu (Kampong Ibol) became fringe dwellers adjoining Kampong Ibol proper, but they remained intact as a community. On the other hand, the communities that were forced off their wet-rice fields by tin mining could not replace their wet-rice fields in the tin-mining regions where wet-rice land was scarce. They were forced to join other established groups in smaller parties and to become more dependent on rubber. The mixed communities of Kampong Baharu (Selim River), Timoh Setesen, Balun Ulu, and Pusing were probably formed in this way.

In some of these Mandailingers were no longer in a majority, and they suffered the erosion of cultural confidence and integrity which is the lot of a minor unit in a social whole which is trying to transform itself.

But, as we have seen, the factor which mainly determined whether the Mandailing community maintained its cultural cohesion was the percentage of members owning wet-rice fields. In short, segmentation was usually an involuntary process as far as the community was concerned and at least one of the resulting units found itself in a different ecological and social milieu possibly without wet-rice fields, was forced to compromise, lost its cultural integrity, and underwent cultural change.

Fragmentation

Fragmentation is an extreme form of segmentation. It may be caused by gross economic disruption such as the advance of tin dredging over the rice fields. A close study of the local history of Kinta would probably reveal that this has happened several times. It may also be caused by economic competition which forces a change of role, for example, there were formerly Mandailing merchant communities at Pusing and Kajang which have disintegrated owing to competition from Chinese traders. (See plates 7 and 8.)

Fragmentation sees the end of a migrant group and the formation of several *merantau*, fortune seeking, social units. In the past forty years none of these have become a new migrant group, rather they have lost their identity in that of an established community, possibly changing their sub-cultural allegiance at the same time, or become fringe dwellers near a market town like Simpang Ampat or Tanjong Rambutan. Here they enter a heterogeneous cultural stream of "modern Malay" in communities in which social identity is determined in universalistic not in familistic terms. There are of course various mixtures of *gemeinschaft* and *gesellschaft* elements[16]—a religious teacher and his elderly in-laws who are owners of rubber gardens, a Mandailing merchant teamed with other non-Chinese (and non-Mandailing) merchants, a schoolteacher whose penumbra of status as an official is shared by members of his family.

Another form of fragmentation is characterized not by the dispersal of small units but by the attrition of younger age grades.

Plate 7.   Retailing: a traditional itinerant Mandailing merchant in a market in Yen District

Plate 8.   Retailing: Chinese shop-houses in Mendaling Street, Kajang, Ulu Langat District, where probably there were formerly traditional Mandailing merchants

When there is no longer any room for local land development a continuous outflow of younger people seeking their fortune leaves a community of aged landowners. Chemor has something of this quality. As a result the community maintains its conservative character, but the culture loses its vitality and integrity because there are not enough persons to fill all the roles necessary to keep the culture going, consequently the remaining members sink into satisfaction and identification with the local scene.

Re-integration

The conception of village organization which the pioneer Mandailingers brought with them to Malaya included the notions of vertical and horizontal segmentation. The vertical segments were lineages and the horizontal ones classes. The *raja* lineage occupied a special place at the top of the hierarchy. It has already been pointed out (chapter 2) that traditional Mandailing leaders in their new role of *Penghulu* in Malaya stimulated the founding of new settlements and acted as their patron. This kind of leadership is historically derived, mythologically supported, and based on a concatenation of kinship relationships. When the fragments of disturbed communities come together these elements are absent and so therefore is traditional leadership. The opportunity to re-form my be provided by the administration, for example on a government-sponsored wet-rice project. A community that is re-forming often attracts attention from the administration because resettlement involves problems of land occupation and in any event the administration must find someone through whom it can deal with the community. This has been done in the past and still is largely done through appointment of a person from the community to act as head; if a good appointment is made, i.e. the appointee proves to be acceptable to the administration and the community, the appointment may stand for many years. The appointee must have some knowledge of customary law in order to have a basis from which to generate the social processes that become characteristic of that community. Decisions on social and economic matters do not spontaneously create new modes of behaviour, they revive and re-formulate old modes of behaviour.[17] Hence it is always likely that the ways of doing things that come to be accepted will be based on the most common elements of customary law.

A community which illustrates these processes is Kg Parit-parit 15-18B (S. Lampam). This was founded on a government-sponsored rice project near Telok Anson in 1939. It now consists of Javanese (10 per cent), Indigenous Malays (9 per cent), Mandailingers (63 per cent), and other Sumatrans (18 per cent). In the Mandailing community there is fairly high use of the Mandailing language, the Generalized Sumatran kinship terminology is used, and there is some knowledge of the characteristic divisions of the Mandailing social system. It was commented in this community that clans have no use in Malaya though they are of use in Sumatra. A member of the community visited Sumatra in 1968 and another member in 1973. This community illustrates the possibility of the creation from heterogenous fragments of a relatively conservative community which remains in a steady state, maintains cultural integrity, and keeps in contact with its cultural mainstream. The point about this community, of course, is that many of its members work wet-rice fields.

Re-integration often depends upon the creation of new kinship ties; a closely related process is the maintenance of the social network by economic ties, by marriage, and by intervisiting, for example, a man who leaves his natal village may still maintain economic ties there through land rights which he does not give up. The most common type of marriage for a Mandailinger in Malaysia is still with another Mandailinger,[18] and many of these marriages make the kinship network denser, particularly between villages in the same area.[19] Visiting relatives in other villages in Malaysia is a popular form of purposeful entertainment. In short the informal information channels through which gossip and news pass provide the culturally significant data by means of which the cultural mainstream is maintained and slowly transformed.

Assimilation

The concept of Modern Malaysia must exist in various forms.[20] There are probably class-linked typologies of attitudes and values, dress, education, wealth, power, and general behaviour, in rural and urban varieties. The problem of trying to decide what is Malay culture has already been discussed (in the Introduction) and dismissed as an academic exercise which becomes a non-problem in the face of the cultural diversity that is the empirical reality. What really matters is what is in the minds of the Malays of West Malaysia, and this is the great unknown that awaits report by Malaysian anthropologists and sociologists.[21] Accordingly as far as the Mandailingers in West Malaysia are concerned, assimilation has to be discussed as a process of cultural loss, which takes various forms according to what non-traditional economic and socio-political roles are taken up.

It is nothing new for Mandailingers to become merchants. This occupation has become traditional since Islamization, indeed there were formerly more Mandailing merchants in West Malaysia than there are now[22] (see plates 7 and 8). A few still take up this occupation and remain in the cultural mainstream, but it is unusual for a Mandailinger to carry out agricultural or semi-skilled work for wages, to cultivate a single cash crop, or to practice fishing.[23]

The Mandailingers have always placed a high value on education and have sent as many of their boys to secondary school as possible. This they have managed to do with greater frequency than other sub-cultural groups as a result of their greater wealth.[24] Many Mandailingers have had successful careers in various departments of the federal government and have retired; others are now following them. A role in administration normally entails residence outside the village and adoption of an urban life-style.[25] Mandailingers have frequently entered service departments such as railways, land, education, and police with headquarters in Kuala Lumpur, and come to live in the capital. There is however no discernible enclave in Kuala Lumpur in which officials of Mandailing origin live. Clearly entry into government service involves at least in theory identification as a Malay and sub-cultural anonymity. Yet on retirement some Mandailingers go to live once more in physical proximity with other Mandailingers. Batu Empatbelas and Sungai Kantan near Kajang are partly made up of Mandailingers who live on their pensions.[26] This suggests that the official role which, while it is occupied, appears to dominate life-style completely is only one determinant of the total pattern of behaviour of the individual. An official can have more than one identity.

The pace of change

The last section raises the question of whether assimilation is a viable concept in a multicultural society in which there is no model culture pattern that individuals might imitate and, moreover, in which the picture is complicated by the existence of social strata within each culture group. There is no official version of the Malay cultural complex as a whole in Malaysia but to the extent that certain segments of Malay culture have been regulated by government decree and others have been subjected to government propaganda there has been an attempt to bring uniformity to some aspects of Malay culture. The most important of these are religion, land rights, and language, and we shall explore the range of free choice still remaining in these areas below. But this administrative rationalization is of quite minor importance in comparison with the effect on Malay attitudes and values of the presence in West Malaysia of large numbers of Chinese and Indians whose culture is viable and actively practised. The effect of this presence on the economic and political context in which culture change in Mandailing communities has taken place has changed several times since the Mandailing communities were founded. We shall now look at the way in which these changes have affected the Mandailingers' consciousness of identity.

The economic context and cultural change

It has already been shown that internal trade conditions can be treated as an external controlled variable with respect to which place a Mandailinger chooses to settle in. This variable has the same status with respect to cultural change in Mandailing communities.

The variable that affects cultural change the most is way of earning a living. When wet rice ceases to be grown, a key element of Mandailing culture disappears. In the early stages of development of Mandailing communities this activity was protected from competition or domination from Chinese and Indians and the preference given to Malays for acquiring land on wet-rice projects appears to have continued after World War II, although the Malays have been competing in some places with Chinese for land for growing other crops.[27] The net effect of this policy of protection has been to maintain isolation and slow down culture change.

The Mandailingers' legal status in Malaysia as Malays effects changes in their culture. This status becomes economically important when resources are short or there is ecological stress, i.e. when segmentation or fragmentation is about to take place people then become more conscious of economic conditions and in this situation a change of identity may be economically advantageous. A new ethos is adopted when such a change occurs because a name which is a shorthand for an identity stands also for a constellation of cultural characteristics, and to play out a new identity "properly" requires a change in life style. In short, ecologically stable conditions encourage isolation and little cultural change, ecologically unstable conditions which bring about segmentation or fragmentation induce psychological changes including the adoption of a new identity.

Political shifts and identification

The Mandailing migrants probably perceived Malaya from the Islamic viewpoint, as a culturally superior region. After Islamization many of the religious teachers in Mandailing were Menangkabau men. But these gradually became incorporated into Mandailing society through marriage and were replaced by Mandailingers, although a number of teachers from outside the area probably continued to visit from time to time.[28] In oral tradition in Mandailing, Menangkabau does not figure as a place to which to go for a religious education, Malaya has this status.

In the twentieth century Mandailing has remained provincial from the point of view of religious education but religious institutions have diversified, penetrated into social life, and come to compete with other institutions. The economic expansion of the early part of the century and the vigour of the Mandailingers as traders enabled many people to go to Mecca. The penetration of Islam took place at the same time as Islamic traders' associations played a role in stimulating anti-colonial movements in the then Dutch East Indies. After the Indonesian Declaration of Independence in 1945 political parties took an interest in both secular and religious education and there was some competition for the minds of the young.

In Malaya, on the other hand, the Mandailingers found themselves in a long-established Islamic polity that could claim its own golden age in the Malacca sultanate. Under the British the sultan was not only nominally the head of each state but he was responsible for religious affairs. Thus after a fashion the situation resembled the classic Islamic pattern, although the daily processes of administration were divorced from religious influence. This suited the pioneers because they could express the economic ethic of Islam in independent action in the economic field and at the same time feel the comfort and brotherliness of an Islamic community and the support of an Islamic head of state. This situation has changed a little since Independence because regulations have been promulgated by the sultans in their role as guardians of religion which have an effect on the structure of village society (for example in relation to marriage payments). This rationalization is a symptom of an attempt to purify religion. In modern times there has been a public confrontation between the proponents of religion and those of customary law, but as far as I can see this had not led to any division in Mandailing communities. As we have seen the customary law that is being followed varies from community to community but no version of it is in strong conflict with Islamic canon law (in contrast with the matrilineal inheritance law of Menangkabau and Negeri Sembilan), consequently as far as the Mandailingers in Malaya are concerned the only effect has been to confirm their identity as Muslims in a Muslim society.

At the time of the movement of the Mandailing community founders to Malaya that Muslim society was under the protection of a foreign power, but the notion of Islamic brotherhood extended the boundaries of social consciousness far beyond the physical boundaries of Malaya to the world-wide community of co-religionists. Yet the Muslims had to recognize that they were members of a special kind of political order in which the real power was not in Muslim hands. Moreover that order was itself fractionated; each state had its own sultan and the local chiefs, although they symbolically submitted to the sultan on ceremonial occasions, exerted their power in their own region much as they pleased.[29] Nevertheless, consciousness of being Muslim carried with it the notion of political hegemony and differentiated the Muslims from the non-Muslims. The latter could be regarded as subordinate peoples who contributed a sense of superiority to Malay identity. The Malays did not see themselves as non-Chinese, they had the more parochial view of the Chinese as non-Muslims.[30]

But in the aftermath of World War II the political ambitions of some Chinese in Malaya were revealed and this sharpened the view that the Malays took of the Chinese. The bland view gave way to a vision of the Chinese as political as well as economic rivals. Hence the British suggestion of 1945 for a Malayan Union in which all residents in Malaya should be regarded equally as citizens in a federal political unit was rejected not only because it conflicted with the view that the Malays took of themselves as lords of the land, but also because the Chinese seemed to have vastly superior economic strength.[31] The rapprochement between Malay, Chinese, and Indian political leaders which resulted in the Alliance Party was a political and economic convenience organized by economically secure non-Malays and the Malay "establishment". At the grass roots level, the effect that this initiative might have had was offset by the picture of the Chinese as responsible for the guerrilla activity of the Emergency.

This changed view of the Malay group's disabilities and functions affected the pace of Malayanization in that Mandailingers could see themselves as having a new commonality with other Malay ethnic groups. Moreover they were driven to redress the economic imbalance by new economic ventures including working for wages. It may have been some sense of a need to defend the Malay world which led numbers of young men to join the police and the army in the 1963-68 period. But this gave way to a more sophisticated search for new economic avenues by migration to towns; and so the pace of change quickened, at least from the behavioural viewpoint.

Malayanization and the future

Reality and dream in government policy on development

To assess the success of the Malaysian government's efforts to use the development programme as an agent of Malayanization, we must look at the difference between official policy and the facts on the ground. The programme itself is based primarily on Western economic thinking. The concentration on agricultural development is presumably intended to improve food production in West Malaysia to the point where that part of the country is self-sufficient in foodstuffs, thus saving foreign exchange, and at the same time to increase the production of cash crops like rubber that earn foreign exchange. The implementation of such a programme clearly depends on adequate coordination and positive reception of the programme by the farmers. Coordination has been attempted by a highly rationalized model for development applied in all areas with progress monitored in a central office in Kuala Lumpur, and the use of the hierarchical system of administrative control inherited from the British. An attempt has been made to introduce some flexibility into the programme and adjust it to local conditions through organized monthly meetings with villagers. In the 1963-68 period these meetings were in effect seen as an opportunity for the district officer or his assistants to persuade the conservative farmers to do what the government wants, but in recent years the government has provided more capital and made less effort to get the villagers to take action for themselves. In the Second Malaysia Plan the government has made clear that it aims to re-structure Malay society, and intends to give special help to *bumiputra*, the sons of the land.

The new economic policy which the Second Malaysia Plan is designed to implement has two "prongs", one is the eradication of poverty among all Malaysians and the other to "correct particularly racial economic imbalance through the modernization of rural life, a rapid and balanced growth of urban activities and the creation of a Malay commercial and industrial community".[32] In practice this means giving aid in the form of training courses, capital, and contracts to *bumiputra*.

In addition to its primarily economic objectives the rural programme therefore carries a load of social and political objectives. It does not rely solely on increasing incomes as a way of keeping the farmer and his sons and daughters on the land but aims to improve the village way of life by the provision of amenities. Some of these amenities serve to intensify the traditional character of the village community, e.g. by providing money for the rebuilding of mosques and shrines, others introduce new elements, e.g. the provision of electricity. Some changes provide more work, e.g. making fish-ponds, others provide for leisure, such as making badminton courts. On the whole the reception of the programme by the farmers is good because the programme is used to maintain or buy allegiance to the party in power and hence there is some response to local demands. But this response does not necessarily introduce a change of perspective on the villager's part. Although it accords well with the Malay idea of the integrity of the village community, the programme is secular and economic in orientation and not emotive and nationalistic, and it does not develop a consciousness of a Malaysian rural way of life which all share it gets only as far as putting new elements into judgments of the comparative advantage of my village versus other villages or judgments of my village context versus an urban context or a Sumatran context.

To particularize this as far as the Mandailingers in Malaysia are concerned, we must look again at the Mandailing ethos. The Mandailing interest in economic advancement is well met by the programme, for example, they can get more land through the fringe alienation schemes, but this does not lead to reinvestment of people in farming, it leads to attempts to achieve a change of family status through more education for the children. There are plenty of models of well-educated Mandailingers who have had a successful career in government service to follow.[33]

Internal movement and rural development

The new settlers on F.L.D.A. and similar state schemes provide an example of role making by government decree. The rules for recruitment, movement, land tenure, and repayment are clear cut. Places are sometimes provided for locals but theoretically applicants can come from anywhere in Malaysia (on F.L.D.A. schemes at least). They must fulfil certain age and experience criteria, await their turn, and take up their place when the administration tells them to do so. In theory an attempt is being made to provide the young and disadvantaged with a viable farming career. In the spirit that leads the government to provide community services under the development programme, meeting halls are built on the settlement areas. From the Mandailing viewpoint this is a process of fragmentation without re-integration, because the mode of choice of settlers makes the assumption that all applicants already *are* Malaysians. It remains to be seen what kind of communities will emerge on these settlements.

As we have seen, another way in which new roles are created by government action is through urbanization following education and training. This route is providing an increasingly popular escape from rural life and hence from commitment to Mandailing culture. Under the Second Malaysia Plan a much wider variety of job opportunities is opening up for young Malays, although it is not yet known how far the Malaysian economy can provide jobs for the increasing numbers of those with a secular education. In present conditions it may well be that the divorce of the educated young from Mandailing culture will be more complete than in the past when kinship ties were often maintained with rural relatives among whom one married. As a result, retirement to a high rise apartment in Kuala Lumpur instead of to a rural retreat like Sungai Kantan may become the rule.

Alternative outcomes of present policies

The struggle for power in the Malaysian countryside between the representatives of parliamentary democracy and the bureaucracy inherited from colonial times is a public presentation of alternative cultural principles—on the one hand, authority with responsibility, on the other, representation and engagement. The first is closer to long-standing Mandailing ideas (and the ideas of Malays generally) about leadership and the distribution of power. But in pioneering Mandailing communities the traditional lines of social segmentation have been broken down as the social concepts which sustained them have been lost.[34] Moreover, there always was in traditional Mandailing culture egalitarianism within and between kinship units and this found expression in the representation of groups on the village council. These ideas are sustained by Islamic ideas about brotherhood and equality. Consequently the notion of an elected headman is not entirely strange to the source ideas of Mandailing culture.[35] But authority over the community has always been a source of irritation to the community. There were two warrants for it: that derived from the break-away system by which new communities were founded, and that derived from Islam. According to the first, the village acknowledged the overlordship of the village of origin, the mother village, and this was expressed by symbolic prestations;[36] according to the second, the village accepted the overlordship of a foreign power. A system of parliamentary democracy cannot be derived from either of these systems. Consequently if the ideas of such a system are to spread they are likely to induce some strain in the culture of Mandailing communities. Parliamentary democracy involves a new kind of self-identity which the villagers may not want.[37] Herein lies a point of comparison with Sumatra. If it persists the system of parliamentary democracy may induce cleavages in Mandailing communities or reinforce cleavages that already exist between the young and the old, the wealthy and the not-so-wealthy, the religious and not-so-religious, and the like.

A second important point of policy that will affect Malayanization is the long-term direction of the rural economy. It has already been shown that the ups and downs of the rubber market had no effect on the pattern of migration to Malaya and in recent years the consistently downward trend has been offset by technical advances which have increased yields for the same amount of effort. But even some of the villagers themselves believe that the future of natural rubber is uncertain.[38]

In some parts of Malaya rubber has been replaced by oil palm, but this had not so far affected any Mandailing community. The requirements of this crop are different from those of rubber. It cannot be economically produced and processed on a small scale as readily as rubber. If they are to grow it smallholders must form cooperatives. This means government intervention and capitalization and the regulation of the economic affairs of farmers by government officials. This is the kind of situation from which many of the founders of the Mandailing settlements in Malaya were trying to escape. Although there has been some cultural change in Mandailing communities since they were founded farmers still have in mind, as the ideal situation, the independent nuclear family household making its own economic decisions. Whenever they have the opportunity farmers diversify their crops.

Cooperatives do not last long; some exist in name but are inactive. There is a rice mill cooperative in only one Mandailing community (near S. Lampam). One other community participates in a rice mill cooperative organized by others. There are two rubber-processing cooperatives in Mandailing communities at present (there were none in 1968 and one in 1963). In short, Mandailingers do not show any capacity for working together for very long.[39] If rubber prices continue to fall therefore, rubber-dependent Mandailing communities are likely to segment or fragment; piecemeal migration to towns or group migration to other areas could result.

In some areas this outflow from the villages might be stopped if more jobs become available in local development projects or industries; in recent years young villagers have shown that they will stay in the village and work for wages outside if the work is available (page 104), but if this happens occupational and economic differences will grow in the village, a number of different interest groups will arise, and there will be what might be called fragmentation in place.

Malays and Chinese

Prior to World War II each of the major ethnic groups in Malaya functioned in its role in the socio-economic order engineered by the British; Chinese political consciousness and pride had been stimulated by the resurgence of China and there had grown among some Chinese a knowledge of Communist principles stemming also from China. There may have been some disquiet amongst Malays at the economic pressure to which they were subjected by some Chinese, but on the whole they relied on the protection of the British. There was no overt inter-ethnic conflict. The Japanese occupation from February 1942 to September 1945 changed this situation. The Japanese saw the Chinese in Malaya as the financial supporters of the Chinese enemy against whom they had been fighting on the Chinese mainland since 1937. They demanded this support for themselves in the form of a "gift" of M$50 million from the Chinese of Malaya and the Straits Settlements. The Communist Chinese formed the Malayan People's Anti-Japanese army which fought a guerrilla war against the Japanese with the logistic support of the Malayan People's Anti-Japanese Union composed of persons who played a dangerous double role in towns and villages. The wealthy Chinese merchants who had been the leaders of the Chinese community withdrew. The Malays, on the other hand, were wooed as the legitimate rulers of Malaya.[40] Malayan police were used against the Chinese guerrillas. In the early days of the British military administration of 1945, the Chinese-inspired leftist organizations made a determined effort to take over the government of the country. This promoted Malay reactions, including attacks on Chinese in different parts of the country, and thus emerged a consciousness of opposition between the two ethnic groups where none had been before.[41]

This consciousness has generated sporadic "incidents" of Malay attacks on the Chinese, a view of the long drawn out Emergency period as a Chinese attack on the Malays, and the civil unrest of 1969. In part the passive attitude of the government towards race relations provided a climate in which hostility emerged whenever there was competition for resources. The formation of an active Department of National Unity may stem from the erosion of confidence in the future integrity of Malaysia, but such a department cannot change people's attitudes quickly, nor can it do away with fundamental facts like population growth and the depletion of resources.

Present government policy reasserts two features of pre-World War II British policy, i.e. the "special position" of the Malays and Malay rulership. After the short-lived attempt by the British after the war to drop these features they were brought into play again, for example in 1952 Sir Gerald Templer announced the policy of admitting one qualified non-Malay to every four Malays and of reserving a certain quota of business licences and scholarships for Malays (dealt with in Popenoe 1970). The *bumiputra*, sons of the land, concept was thus extended from the field of land tenure into the general economy and projected into political thinking. The conceptual origins of this idea were present in the 1940s; Noone (1948), for example, speaking of his experiences in the field in 1940 says that the term *orang Melayu* (Malay person) as then used covered a population acknowledging one creed but of diverse physical and cultural origins; he saw regional variations (amongst Malays) as considerable though not at that time sufficiently appreciated, except in regard to dialects.[42] Some commentators have emphasized, if not over-emphasized, the regional variations. It has been suggested that the view of the Malays as natives of the land is paradoxical, that it is permissible to question whether "the Malays" are really native people or immigrants (Dagli 1951). The view was even put forward in the British period; Wilkinson (1923), for example, said "there is no such thing as a true Malay racial type and the expression 'real Malay' must be used guardedly". Vlieland (1934), who was conscious of the political convenience of regarding all Malays as belonging to the one people, said, "The Malay, whose real home is in Sumatra, not the Peninsula ... is habitually accepted as 'a native of the country and owner of the soil' without inconvenient enquiry." These unpopular thoughts are echoed today with reference to the *bumiputra* idea, but have apparently done little to stem the progress of the *bumiputra* movement. The First *Bumiputra* Congress was held in 1965, and its main effect was to get more technical training provided for Malays; the Second *Bumiputra* Congress held in 1968 extended Malay privileges in a practical way by creating jobs for *bumiputra*; the congress required a 50 per cent share in all public companies to be reserved for Malays; trading companies to be encouraged to appoint *bumiputra* as agents; all government contracts to go to *bumiputra* if their bid was no more than 10 per cent above the lowest tender; and mining dredges to appoint *bumiputra* as 50 per cent of their staff and gravel pumps 25 per cent.[43] A share in the prosperity accompanying the development of Malaya has been ensured for Malays by requiring companies that receive a tax incentive to employ a substantial proportion of Malays.

By adopting these and other measures the government is attacking some of the bases of ethnicity.[44] The Second Malaysia Plan aims explicitly at forcing a breakout of the Malays from their economic and occupational encapsulation; the use of Malay as the national language has been pushed ahead in spite of opposition and this has apparently reduced the linguistic differentiation of the population;[45] but religiously and socially Malaysia remains divided.

Some Chinese have adapted themselves to the present policies and retain their belief in their own ability to survive, economically, better than the Malays. The rural Malays, as Wilson (1967) found, regard rice growing, gardening, fishing, collecting firewood, and sometimes cooking and clothes washing as work, *kerja*, and other economic activities, including rubber tapping, as money making, *bikin duit*, an activity which they supposedly despise.[46] Hence some Chinese believe that they can incorporate the Malays into a Chinese-dominated economic system by using Malays as front men or pay them off for privileges;[47] this may well work for a time in some sections of commerce, but two new factors, among many, have to be reckoned with: the competition from the public sector of commerce and industry which the government controls, and the emergence of common interests among Chinese, Malay and Indian workers.[48] But even more important to the Chinese is the less obvious attack on their cultural integrity that the idea of the New Malaysia represents.[49] The Islamization of the Chinese population must surely be in view, even if distantly, and the learning by Chinese primary school children of the Jawi script for the writing of the Malay language is a step in this direction. Whether the Chinese can be quietly converted remains to be seen.[50]

The Mandailingers may have to face a future in which Malay political power is purely symbolic and the real direction of the country is in the hands of Chinese entrepreneurs or alternatively a future in which there is a constant threat of Chinese insurrection[51] and these possibilities must have a great potency for most of them because they live in a part of the country in which the Chinese are in numerical superiority.[52]

Investment and identification with Malaysia

The founders of the traditional village of Kerangai brought with them from Sumatra rice seeds and money. Presumably the money was for buying rice fields. Three kinds of sweet rice[53] and five of ordinary rice were brought. It is significant that these pioneers brought with them the key to their spiritual, social, and physical survival. The spirit of the rice is the most important element of cultural ecology in Mandailing. But this rice is now finished and so has died presumably the magical connection with the home village. What remains is a cultural similarity which can generate bonds of sympathy but not of interdependence.

More durable are kinship connections, which have a personalized quality. Many of the present members of the Mandailing communities in Malaysia had fathers or mothers who were born in Mandailing, and must have uncles, aunts, and cousins still living there. Of course these relationships are optative because of the distance involved and the relevant obligations can be ignored with impunity.[54]

Growing from kinship connections are economic bonds with the homeland engendered through the ownership of land in common by patrilineal kinsmen. But even in Mandailing itself, land is no longer worked in common by this group as it used to be, although the principle of ownership in common is maintained and is sometimes used to prevent the breakup of an estate on the ground that absent kinsmen have not all been accounted for or consulted. But I know of no Mandailinger in Malaysia who openly lays claim to land in Sumatra, although in principle there must be land in his village of origin to which many a Mandailinger in Malaysia could make some claim of usufruct. In short, magical connection, economic obligations, cultural similarities, and kinship ties die out and probably in that order, and as they go, the bonds of the Mandailing community with its homeland are reduced.

In Malaysia, on the other hand, the Mandailing community develops and changes in accordance with its local context and helps to transform it. In the tin-bearing and rubber-growing areas of Selangor and Perak, the Sumatran immigrants of the last hundred years are in such numerical superiority that it is they who constitute the Malay population. Up until World War II, each sub-ethnic group lived in relative social and cultural isolation and some communities still do. But since the Japanese occupation there has been disruption of the homeland visiting pattern and a breakdown of cultural isolation in Malaysia. It is the Sumatran groups themselves who now constitute the cultural patchwork of Selangor and Perak and whose shades of difference often go unrecognized by the administration itself. As far as the Mandailing communities are concerned, they could live in Malaysia and conform to local cultural demands while maintaining their cultural integrity by practising *adat rantau*, the custom of fortune hunting.

According to this system, the individual recognizes that, for the purpose of making his fortune, he should follow local custom, at least outwardly. Implicit in this idea is the widely held notion that the community has its own rules to which those who wish to live in it should conform. An individual practising local custom for convenience can maintain intact the constellation of characteristics of his culture of origin and use this as a cultural yardstick. Thus there are Mandailingers in Malaysia who say that the notion of *marga* and *suku*, traditional lineal kinship concepts, are not useful in Malaysia, but can be used in Sumatra. This is the double standard of a bicultural individual. Other persons say that there are no social rules in Malaysia, i.e. that their own rules are absent (*disini t'ada rul*). The attitude of the fortune hunter is shown by those persons who say that they obey the official regulations in order to keep out of trouble (*ikut resmi tanah Melayu inilah*). Still other persons maintain bi-cultural standards but regard traditional Mandailing custom as of the past, and contemporary practice as up-to-date; people who come from Sumatra, they say, use Sumatra rules, others use rules of modern times (*saman modern*). In all these ways, persons maintain bicultural standards; they know of two ways of acting, two ways of behaving in particular situations. They practise the mode of behaviour which best serves their interests. This is the essence of *adat rantau*.

In the course of time an individual practising local culture for his own convenience may come to feel satisfied with that culture and accept it as his own. I do not know how long this process takes, but it seems likely that such a change takes place when the individual has succeeded in making his fortune and that fortune is in material goods such as rubber gardens and rice-fields. It is then easy to settle down in a context which has become familiar and over which the successful man can exert some control. Another form of investment is in a good education for one's children with a view to their taking a job in the administration, but as we have seen, an official position does not mean a complete loss of sub-cultural identity.

Comparative advantage and future migration

The thesis has been put forward that the intending Mandailing migrant judges whether he will move or not according to a principle of comparative advantage. To forecast the likely movements of the Mandailingers in Malaysia, we must therefore compare, from the Mandailing viewpoint, the areas in which they live with areas to which they could move. The latter are most likely to be the towns and villages of West Malaysia or the rural areas of Sumatra.[55] The former are readily accessible but success there is not easy for an un-educated farmer because entrepreneurial activities are dominated by the Chinese who employ few Malays. In Sumatra, on the other hand, the farmer can regenerate his claims to usufruct of land and the would-be trader has relatively little competition from the Chinese. Sumatra undoubtedly offers better opportunities for small-scale trading, and it may be that if some Mandailingers in Malaysia decide to try their hand at this traditional occupation, they will move to Sumatra to do it. But what about farming? At the present time, the technical and financial help available to farmers in West Malaysia far outstrips the aid given by the Indonesian government in the Mandailing homeland. The general living conditions in Malaysia are also superior: roads are in better shape; access to towns and markets is freer; piped water and better health facilities are available in more villages. In a material sense, the Mandailingers in Malaysia are clearly better off—they have better houses, more furniture, and more radios and other electrical equipment; a few farmers in Malaysia own generators, refrigerators, and motor cars, no farmer in Sumatra owns such things. Under present conditions it is unlikely that any Mandailinger in Malaysia would want to move back to Sumatra. But for the future, other aspects must be con-sidered. There is no pressure from the Chinese in Sumatra, but pres-sure from the Chinese could well increase in Malaysia. The fact that some Malays in Malaysia see the extermination of the Chinese as the appropriate ultimate solution to the Chinese problem is an in-dication of the desperation that some Malays feel.

If the objectives of the Second Malaysia Plan are reached, the disparity between Malays and Chinese in economic opportunities will be much reduced but for the Muslim Mandailingers to accept the non-Muslim Chinese as Malaysian brothers would require a reversal of attitudes. It seems more likely that the Mandailingers will continue to keep open an escape route to their homeland by maintaining their double identity.

Notes to text

INTRODUCTION

1. Malayanization so defined is a sub-species of culture change in general. It can be distinguished from government efforts to introduce a new identity for all citizens as Malaysians (see Tan Sri Data Muhammad Ghazali bin Shafie, *The New Malaysian*, 1971).

CHAPTER ONE: THE MALAYSIAN CONTEXT

1. In recent times there have been cross-Straits ferries from Belawan (Medan) to Penang and from Dumai to Malacca.
2. Cowan (1968) sees the history of maritime Southeast Asia in terms of a struggle between a land-based power in Java and a maritime power based in the Straits area. Within this larger picture Straits powers have alternated between internal development and outward expansion. From the seventh to the ninth centuries the various Srivijaya dynasties controlled the Straits first from Java and later from Palembang, Acheh, and Kedah. They were succeeded by Jambi and then in the fourteenth century by the last Hindu Javanese empire of Majapahit. The latter was too far away to exert effective control of the Straits which fell to a Pasai-Kedah combination and finally to Malacca, which in the fourteenth century conquered the whole of Malaya south of Kedah and subjugated the areas of Lokan, Indragiri, Kampar and Liak across the Straits in Sumatra. During the next century and a half the Portuguese tried to control the Straits by seapower based on Malacca; they were challenged by the Dutch who blockaded the Straits from a base in Johore and by a trade-hungry Acheh which took the opportunity to span the Straits and overrun Johore, Pahang, Perak, and Kedah. After capturing Malacca in 1740 the Dutch also attempted to control the Straits by seapower, although they maintained a liaison with Johore which had possessions on the Sumatran side. The British set up a rival port at Penang in 1786, forced the decline of Malacca and got rid of Dutch influence in Johore by the establishment of Singapore. In 1824 the Anglo-Dutch Treaty of London allotted Malaya to Great Britain and Sumatra to the Dutch as spheres of influence. The last political links across the Straits, the Johore empire and the ties between the Bugis of Selangor and the Bugis of Riau, were severed. The continuing importance of the Straits as a passageway from the Indian Ocean to the China Sea is reflected in the current attempts by Malaysia and Indonesia to control international sea traffic through them.
3. An outstanding example is the role of Acheh as a centre for the dissemination of Islam in the fourteenth century.
4. The Europeans were not culturally important until the nineteenth century. According to one author the Portuguese and the Dutch "made no impact whatsoever on the immediate hinterland of the settlement at Melaka". (Zaharah binti Haji Mahmud 1970,p. 82.)
5. The piracy and slave trade of the Indian archipelago. *Journal of the Indian Archipelago and Eastern Asia* 4 (1850): 46.

6. The Paderis were members of an Islamic revivalist movement initiated in Menangkabau just south of Mandailing in Sumatra by religious teachers who had visited Mecca. The Paderi armies went northwest into Mandailing with the object of converting the population to Islam.
7. See Zaharah binti Haji Mahmud, 1966.
8. Zaharah binti Haji Mahmud adds: "Kedah ... had little to offer the industrious immigrant in the form of a mining economy and other developments associated with such an economy were likewise non-existent." (Ibid., p. 111.)
9. Ibid., p. 109.
10. The *lampan* was a four-sided wooden tray used in washing the tin. According to Jackson (1963, p. 105) the work "was probably carried out by debt bondsmen and slaves of the chiefs"
    An exception to these small-scale mines has been recorded. Towards the end of the eighteenth century Malays built a large embankment to block the Selangor river; "at both ends of this embankment long sluices were dug each about one mile long and from 3 inches to 10 feet deep running into the Selangor River. The earth dug out of the mine was thrown into the sluices instead of being piled up as was the custom later." "This was one of the few mines which had been worked by the Malays on a gigantic scale, using a comparatively large capital at this early period." (Abdul Rahman Jalan 1954, pp. 2-3.)
11. Wong Lin Ken and Wong 1960.
12. The opening of the mines at Ulu Kelang illustrates the interplay between initiative and resources. "At some time, perhaps before 1860, Sumatran Malays began to wash for tin at Ulu Klang. But this was a very minor effort. In 1857 Raja Abdullah of Klang and Raja Juma'at of Lukut persuaded two Chinese merchants of Malacca to provide supplies and credit to the amount of $30,000. They then sent 87 Chinese miners from Lukut up the Klang River to prospect for tin. Within a month of their arrival only 18 of the miners remained but the work went on." (Gullick 1955, p.10.)
13. Winstedt and Wilkinson 1934, p.100.
14. Traditional kin group leaders.
15. The breakdown may have been due to the structure of the state: "The manner in which the greater state was referred to in Malay history ... indicates that basically it was not a unitary state, but an agglomeration of unitary riverine settlements each of which was a highly autonomous unit." (Khoo Kay Kim 1967, p.9.) The same author (p.23) suggests that instead of internal decay the system in the third quarter of the nineteenth century had deteriorated because of exploitation of weaknesses by "ambitious economic groups".
16. Sheppard 1961.
17. Gullick 1960, p. 58.
18. Willer 1849.
19. There seem to have been several kinds of relationships between Chinese and local Malay authorities: trade alliances actively promoted by Malay chiefs; mutual exploitation where attempts were made to get more taxes or to increase a concession under conditions of close contact between chief and miners; and relationships of convenience which were negotiated by "Foreign" Malays who acted as intermediaries. The kind of Chinese-Malay disagreement that might occur is illustrated by the story of Raja Busu who controlled an area of the Lukut fields where a tax of 10 per cent was at first put on tin exports. Attempts were made to raise the tax from time to time and one night in 1834 the Chinese miners appeared before Raja Busu's house to renegotiate the tax. They found a large amount of tin stacked near the house, became jealous, and threatened to burn down the house unless Raja Busu came down from the house to meet them. His reply was "Muslims are not afraid to die; do what you like". The house was burnt down and the inmates massacred (Khoo Kay Kim 1967). The Chinese secret societies had a wide influence and in some places affected the structure of the total society. In Malacca for example "Malays, Boyanese and Indians" are said to have applied for membership (Khoo Kay Kim 1967, p. 42).
20. See Gullick 1958, p. 115.

21. Moorhead 1963, p. 192. The first British company, the Gopeng Mining Company which worked in an area with many Sumatran migrants, was floated in 1892 (Simms 1968, pp. 74-79).
22. Chai 1967, p. 135.
23. Ding Eing Tan Soo Hai 1963, p.43.
24. In Perak and Selangor, the main target areas for Mandailing migrants, there was a rice shortage from early in the nineteenth century when the tin industry began to expand. In the Kerian area Tunku Mentri of Larut dug a ditch 13 kilometres long before British intervention. In 1880 this was widened and deepened, larger works were mooted in 1890, and the Kerian irrigation scheme was officially opened in 1906. In Selangor in 1910 the area under rice was still only 1,620 hectares. This expanded to 6,480 hectares by 1920 (when the rubber area was 165,645 hectares) but at that time there was more dry rice grown than wet rice; the price of rice was high, but it was not possible to expand the wet-rice area without constructing large drainage channels (see Ahmad bin Sa'adi 1960). In Kedah on the other hand, where there was little tin, rubber was slow to get going; in 1911 99.5 per cent of the Malay population was still engaged in rice production on a subsistence basis (Sharom Ahmat 1970, p. 1).
25. Malay Reservation Enactment 1933.
26. Ding Eing Tan Soo Hai 1963, p. 16.
27. There was the Malayan Civil Service and the Malay Administrative Service. The latter was exclusively "for Malays of royal birth or the Malay aristocracy who received their education culminating with a Cambridge School Certificate from the Malay College, Kuala Kangsar, and later graduates of Raffles College, Singapore and Malay graduates from British Universities". (Danapaul Saveri Dass 1960-61.) Some Malays were promoted from the M.A.S. to the M.C.S. There were five promotions in 1928, eleven in 1932, and twenty in 1937.
28. Maurice Freedman (1960) says that British control "bureaucratized the Rulers and their chiefs. It raised the Ruler from his traditional status as a chief among equals to that of an elevated king; at the same time it turned him into a kind of constitutional monarch."
29. The Malay elite were also protected from competition since, despite repeated requests, the M.A.S. was not opened to non-Malays.
30. Oliver Popenoe (1970) deals with marginality and social cohesion as sources of entrepreneurship in Southeast Asia.
31. Wang Gungwu 1961.
32. The distribution of occupations in Singapore demonstrates that Malays are not unwilling to take up occupations other than farming; only 10 per cent of the population are farmers and fisherman; a percentage only slightly higher than the percentage of farmers among the Chinese (see Warwick Neville 1966, pp. 236-53).

CHAPTER TWO: THE IMMIGRATION AND SETTLEMENT OF MANDAILINGERS

1. There are relics of the Hindu kingdom of Panai in Padang Lawas, the northern part of the Mandailing area (see Schnitger 1937).
2. The Rawa, the immediate neighbours of the Mandailing to the south, are described as "the same people who, passing year by year through our Malacca territories into the middle of the Malay Peninsula, have already established themselves in such strength in the interior of Pahang as almost to set at defiance the power of its ruler the Bindahara." (The piracy and slave trade of the Indian Archipelago 1849, p. 366n.)
3. Willer (1849) asserts that "during the [Paderi] war it frequently happened that whole communities remained for months in the wilderness without houses, salt, or other food than leaves, roots and wild fruits".
4. Willer (1849) describes the upland valleys of Mandailing as a "favoured region" (where) "the greatest prosperity has reigned for some years". He mentions also

that growing of coffee as "a first development of industry". He mistakes as a sign of prosperity the "superabundance of children" that later no doubt became the migrant pool (p. 372). The more mountainous parts of Mandailing however he describes in less salubrious terms as "high and naked mountains ever which the *lalang* (Imperator cylindrica) again spreads its monotonous mantle, where hamlets and cultivated tracts appear to be struck on frightful steeps, where unfruitfulness and poverty have established their hungry seat" (p. 572). It was from this part that the first Mandailing migrants to Malaya came.

5. Sutan Puasa (his title indicates that he was of *raja* stock) was a Mandailinger whose activities in Malaya are of special interest because he was responsible in part for the founding of Kuala Lumpur, the federal capital of Malaysia. He was one of "the more adventurous traders" who moved from Lukut to Ampang to deal in supplies for the mines when mining was started there around 1859 (Middlebrook 1951). He persuaded two Chinese traders with whom he had had dealings in Lukut to come to Ampang and they set up shop at the junction of the Kelang and Gombak rivers at a place that became known as Kuala Lumpur. Hiu Siew became the first Capitan China, according to Middlebrook, with the assistance of Sutan Puasa who obtained the support of the local Malays. Later when Yap Ah Loy was nominated as Capitan China Sutan Puasa pacified rival claimants. He supported Yap Ah Loy in his political struggles by supplying Malay fighting men, and Yap Ah Loy helped him to collect debts by supplying Chinese supporters at the right time. He led Malay fighting men in support of Yap Ah Loy in 1870 and 1872 when Syed Mashhor attacked Kuala Lumpur, but on the latter occasion changed sides. When Kuala Lumpur was retaken by Yap Ah Loy in March 1873 Sutan Puasa disappeared from the scene, only to re-establish himself among the Sumatran population around Cheras and Kajang to the south of Kuala Lumpur, where he became known as a rebel. Yap Ah Loy had his revenge when his forces and those of H.C. Syers, a British appointed military policeman, captured his fort at Kajang and Sutan Puasa was sent to Kelang gaol for some months. He was released in August 1876 and was known as a trader in Kuala Lumpur in 1884.

6. Quoted in Winstedt 1934, p. 22.

7. Gullick 1958, p. 31. Ironworking is a traditional Mandailing specialism. A village with a group of ironsmiths still existed in Upper Mandailing, Sumatra, in 1956.

8. Gullick 1960, p. 76. The presence in the Ulu Langat area of a number of Mandailing communities claimed to be of long standing indicates that these "Sumatrans" probably included Mandailingers.

   According to Ramsay the impetus for the settlement of Menangkabau and Mandailing immigrants in the Kajang area "is said to have been given by the well known Kinnersley brothers who came from Ceylon and were pioneer planters, first of coffee and then of rubber ... They [the Sumatrans] were first employed on felling contracts and then established themselves as smallholders." (Ramsay 1956, pp. 119-24.)

9. Part-time tin washing was still practised in some areas however; stream tin was found "literally everywhere in Kinta; it is worked out of the sand in the river beds—a very favourite employment with Mandheling women; Kinta natives do not affect it much, although there is more than one stream where a good worker can earn a dollar a day." (Hale 1885.)

10. However, according to statistics assembled by Tunku Shamsul Bahrin (1967) the flow of other Indonesian migrants did not cease. A total of 102,545 "Other Malaysians" was recorded in the 1947 census, all of whom were direct migrants from Indonesia. "This figure represented one-third of the total Indonesian population in Malaya in 1947. Out of this total more than 50 per cent arrived in Malaya between 1911 and 1930 and another 31 per cent between 1931 and 1947."

11. Specialization to meet the needs of travelling strangers of a certain cultural group is common. In Mecca there are religious teachers who cater for particular culture groups; in Kuala Lumpur there is a hotel which specializes in catering for Japanese fieldworkers, and, no doubt, in "Pulau Penang" there was a special house at which Mandailingers could spend a comfortable and informative night or

two. There is now no Mandailing community there so far as I have been able to discover.

12. For these details of local history at Gopeng I am indebted to Inche Abdul Rahman bin Imam Awang, a son-in-law of Haji Dollah and a resident of Sungai Itek.

13. In Sumatra the smallest administrative unit above the village was the *kuria*, often composed of a mother-child village complex. The head of the *kuria* was an indigenous *raja* who had the dual role of head under customary law and officer of the Dutch administration.

14. Of the fourteen villages for which information is available the reasons given are: to get land, 5; to get money by felling trees, contracts, etc., 3; for trade, 2; administrative pressure in Sumatra, 2; excessive taxes and demands for corvee labour, 2.

   According to Voon Phin Keong (1967, pp. 43-49) government land policy in Malaya in the mid 1890s favoured the development of estates and smallholders were not allowed to plant alongside roads. This may account for the distribution of settlements established at that time. But from 1909 smallholdings were established on a large scale and there was a second "boom" in 1916. In Ulu Selangor the area planted in rubber smallholdings increased twentyfold from 1908 to 1918.

15. In Kedah traditional Malay markets still flourish.

16. The objective of the early Mandailing settlers at this village was to make money. After selling their garden they went to Mecca and then returned to Sumatra; they were ashamed to return to Sumatra without first going to Mecca.

CHAPTER THREE: CULTURAL CHANGE IN MANDAILING COMMUNITIES: ECONOMY AND LANGUAGE

1. This assumption would be correct for 1955-56 when the author carried out fieldwork in Upper and Lower Mandailing.

2. A few villages may have had shifting cultivation only.

3. There were also special kinship terms of address and reference for mother's brother and mother's brother's son and for father's sister and father's sister's daughter.

4. This type of marriage took two forms: *tangko na golap*, when the girl's father did not know she was to be abducted; and *tangko binoto*, when the girl's father was made aware beforehand that the girl was to be abducted and tacitly gave his consent.

5. The ways in which these customary law marriage payments are combined with the Islamic marriage payment *mahar* are discussed in Tugby (1959).

6. *Sepak raga* is so-called "Malay football" played with a wickerwork ball on a small ground.

7. In the Ulu Langat District for example there are group settlement schemes totalling about 1,175 hectares, a controlled alienation scheme of 1,278 hectares, and fringe alienation schemes of about 46 hectares. In Ulu Selangor District there are four federal development schemes, two state group settlement schemes, seven controlled alienation schemes, and a fringe alienation scheme. In Mukim Behrang Ulu, in the southern part of Batang Padang District where there are three Mandailing communities there are a number of small fringe alienation schemes, a new reservoir for a group settlement scheme which will eventually cover 253 hectares, a 4 hectare experimental double cropping plot, and four cheap housing schemes. Around the village of Jelai in Larut District there are six controlled alienation schemes, three for rubber and *dusun* (orchard) totalling 395 hectares, two for rice totalling 234 hectares, and one for *dusun* of 49 hectares.

8. Two villages, Simpang Sekolah and Tebing Tinggi, in which there are fewer than five Mandailing families and in which the Mandailing component accounts for less than 5 per cent of the total population have been excluded in calculating these figures.

9. Nine sub-cultural groups from Sumatra have been recognized.
10. There is a tendency for indigenous Malays to outnumber other Sumatrans in rubber-dominated villages and vice versa in wet-rice growing villages.
11. The rate of ownership for cars and motor cycles increases in wet-rice growing villages as the number of persons owning wet-rice fields decreases.
12. This account of the minor crops is based on information from eight rubber-dominated villages and ten wet-rice growing villages.
13. This section on wet rice is based on reports from eight wet-rice growing villages and one rubber-dominated village.
14. Swift (1965, p. 48) reports that in Jelebu, Negeri Sembilan, the husband-wife team is the cultivating unit; Jin-Bee Ooi (1963, p. 237) says of "Malaya" that the "farmer" (presumably a man) does the hoeing and that women transplant; and Cooke (1961, pp. 23-4) that transplanting is done almost exclusively by women (though she also mentions that men help with the pruning of the seedlings and transport them to the fields), reaping by women using the *tuwai* (the *sabit* she mentions as being used when the crop is even), and that threshing is done by men. Ding Eing Tan Soo Hai (1963, p. 10) mentions that reaping is done by women using the *tuwai*. Wilson (1967, p. 99), who worked in villages whose population consisted of Sumatran migrants, including one or two Mandailingers, in Selangor, reports that everyone cooperates in clearing the land and in planting, that women and children guard the growing rice from birds, that everyone helps at the harvest, and that women and children winnow and pack the grain. This last report accords fairly well with my own findings from the same area. It is likely that practices differ from area to area and even from sub-cultural group to sub-cultural group within the same village.
15. The mechanical diggers are the equivalent of the buffalo and plough which was used by men in the flatter parts of the Mandailing area of Sumatra until the buffaloes were killed and eaten during the Japanese occupation of World War II.
16. I was told by a Malay official that he could recognize the Mandailingers in his area because they spoke English with a Mandailing "twang"!
17. The "complete dominance of Malaysian dialects among Malaysians" and dialectical differences among Chinese and Indians in Singapore are mentioned by Neville (1966).

CHAPTER FOUR: CULTURAL CHANGE IN MANDAILING COMMUNITIES: SOCIAL ORGANIZATION

1. Kinship terms for aunts, uncles, and some cousins are shown in figure 1.
2. This analysis is based on information from thirteen wet-rice growing communities and eight rubber-dominated communities. Terms of reference have been used for the most part, but when they were not recorded terms of address have been used. Since the latter are usually curtailed forms of the former, e.g. *pa'mentua*, if we have erred at all we have erred on the side of caution.
3. So called because it is similar to the terminology used in the traditional Perak village of Pasir Panjang Laut in the Dindings area.
4. In the fifth village in which Traditional Mandailing is used, the terminology is breaking down, although this village has 61 per cent Mandailingers and 41 per cent of the population own wet-rice fields.
5. The term *pupu* is used by the Singapore Malays (Djamour 1959, p.23) to refer to cousins on either side; *sa-pupu*, one *pupu*, means first cousin, *dua pupu*, two *pupu*, second cousin, and so on. The Petani Malays use the same terms (Fraser 1960, p.125). *Pupu* is infrequently used by the Mandailingers.
6. This result was reached by constructing a matrix showing which terms were known village by village N = 26. It was found that, when the marginal order of the terms was *anak boru, mora, marga,* and *kahangi,* there were only two reversals in the matrix, namely, two villages in which *marga* disappeared before *mora*.
7. It is not possible to separate non-traditional wet-rice villages and rubber villages because there are too little data for the former.

8. The non-Mandailing groups from which Mandailing men in non-traditional and rubber-dominated villages have taken brides include: Kedah Malays, Petani Malays, Rawa, Javanese, Perak Malays, Roken, Selangor Malays, Pahang Malays, Tambuse, Penang Malays, Palembang, Arab, and Selayang. Mandailing women have married Bila, Menangkabau, Negeri Sembilan, Benkahulu, and Banjar men. Of the groups listed only the Menangkabau show any tendency to marry among themselves.

9. As far as I know surrender marriage is unknown among the Mandailingers in Sumatra who would solve the problem by capturing the girl.

10. In the regulations for Selangor that came into force in 1968 the following grades of payment were recognized: Putri Sultan (daughters of the sultan) M$2,500 (formerly M$1,500); Putri Raja Muda dan Putri kepada Putra2 Sultan yang bergelar (daughters of the "young" *raja* and daughters of the titled sons of the sultan) M$2000 (formerly M$1,000); Putri kerabat2 (daughters of the royal family) M$1,000 (formerly M$500); Putri Anak2 Raja (daughters of a *raja*) M$550 (formerly M$400); Anak perampuan Orang2 Besar (children of the sultan's representatives) M$300 (formerly M$200); Cuci Orang2 Besar (grandchildren of sultan's representatives) M$200 (formerly M$100); Anak perampuan orang2 kebanyakan (daughters of commoners) M$80 (formerly M$44). These figures are for previously unmarried girls; for widows the figures are one-quarter of those given except for those who are the daughters of commoners for whom the figure is M$40.

11. *Wang antaran* (Singapore).

12. The details of the ceremonies do probably differ from village to village. In some communities with high Mandailing language usage, the speeches at the wedding ceremony are made in Mandailing if both the partners to the wedding are of Mandailing origin.

13. The exception is a village founded by a religious teacher in which the influence of Islam is very strong; in this village it is said that post-wedding residence can be with parents of either side.

14. All the Mandailingers in Malaya had been Islamized by the time of the period of attraction. They had available to them the Islamic modes of divorce of the Shafite code of canon law.

15. Under Islamic canon law a man is responsible for providing housing, food, and clothing for his wife and children. Quarrels about household upkeep are reportedly the most important immediate cause of divorce. Other common reasons are inability to agree and jealousy on the part of the wife.

16. According to reports in Pasir Panjang Laut, Perak.

17. A will prevents any part of the inheritance going to Bait Ullah, the central Islamic fund into which the property of a man who dies intestate can sometimes pass.

18. There are eight villages in which a Neo-Malayan or Personalized kinship terminology is used. In two of these Islamic canon law is used, in four equal divisions of the inheritance among the children, and for two information is lacking. The association between Neo-Malayan or Personalized kinship terminology and equal division is therefore quite strong.

19. In Islamic theology *jihin* are intelligent beings (of which the other two classes are angels and mankind) who were created from smokeless flame. In pre-Islamic Arabia they were hostile spirits and most Mandailingers also believe that they have this nature.

20. In one rubber-dominated village the grave of the local holy man is visited by Chinese who burn joss sticks there, but not by the local Malays. In Chemor my enquiries about *keramat* aroused laughter which might conceal uncertainty.

21. The head of one traditional village died in 1967 after many years in office and was succeeded by his son.

CHAPTER FIVE: NATION BUILDING: THE FORMAL CONTEXT OF MALAYANIZATION

1. It was also in line with the conservative character of Malay nationalism before

World War II which was, as Soenarno (1960) puts it, "embedded in the feudal social structure". Economic diversification scarcely touched the protected Malay rural communities from which could be generated not a mass movement but only a followship for the British educated traditional leaders.

2. Many Chinese squatters and some Malays were moved during this period into New Villages some of which formed multiracial communities, but after the Emergency the New Villages were perceived to be Chinese communities and this is what they are now.

3. Wilson (1967), speaking of Jendram Hilir, a village of Sumatran immigrants in Selangor, says: " ... during the time of confrontation the attitude of villagers to Indonesia was far from belligerent. In spite of constant radio propaganda, police road blocks and armored cars patrolling through the village, the general opinion in the coffee shop was that Indonesians and Malays would not fight one another (they were *saudara*, even *keluarga*, i.e. kinsmen)." This sentiment was in line with the ideas of Sukarno who stated at a meeting to discuss the extent of Indonesian territory just before the Japanese handover at the end of World War II: "Indonesia will not become strong and secure unless the whole Straits of Malacca is in our hands. If only the west coast of the Straits of Malacca, it will mean a threat to our security." During Confrontation this statement was published by the Malaysian Federal Department of Information in "Background to Indonesia's policy towards Malaysia" (Kuala Lumpur, 1964, quoted in Tepper, 1965, p. 113), but, as far as Indonesian immigrants in West Malaysia were concerned, the statement could not have been interpreted in the same threatening light as the Malaysian government intended.

4. Almost all road notices, for example, are in Malay. The government has supported the Dewan Bahasa dan Pustaka as a national language publishing centre and at the new National University (Universiti Kebangsaan) teaching in almost all subjects is in Malay.

5. The most tragic acts of violence took place in Kuala Lumpur following the Malaysian elections of 1969. These did not spread to the countryside but they resulted in the declaration of martial law which was maintained for eighteen months.

6. Now transformed into the National Front.

7. The district and assistant district officers are well paid. There are two classes of officers and several scales of pay. State officers serve only in their own state. Malaysian Civil Service Officers may serve anywhere in Malaysia or overseas. Some examples of pay scales are: M.C.S. with honours degree, M$750-1,800 per month on time scale with scale G beginning at M$2,000 per month and proceeding eventually to scale D at M$2,500 per month. Allowances such as entertainment and transport are paid and cheap housing is provided.

8. As a first class magistrate a district officer can inflict a fine of up to M$3,000 or a term of six months gaol (an assistant district officer as a second class magistrate can inflict a fine of up to M$500 or one month in gaol). But this is only one aspect of the district officer's work; he is likely to perform also the roles of registrar of marriages and adoptions, chairman of the local town board, chairman of the district rural development committee and collector of inland revenue; he is responsible for the salaries and working conditions of local officers, exercises a coordinating role for all departments, and represents the state and federal governments as necessary. Nowadays the functions of the district office are being divided into three main parts: land administration, rural development and general administration. One investigator has found that local non-administrative elites play a crucial role in decisions made by administration (Singh Satwant Ahluwalia 1970, p.167); my own experience has been that effective day-to-day action in the district office still turns on the personality of the district officer. Some district officers receive a large number of supplicants about all sorts of matters and have to work unofficial hours to get through their ordinary business.

9. Formerly indigenous Malays had a distinct advantage in gaining appointments to *Penghulu*ships, but nowadays *Penghulu*ships are achieved offices; I have met a *Penghulu* who originated from a Banjar group, i.e from the sub-cultural group

generally regarded of relatively low status in West Malaysia.

10. I heard of one council which consisted of twelve elected Chinese and two Malays nominated by the administration.

11. Expenditure on agriculture and rural development rose from an estimated $M411.1 million in the 1961-5 period to a target of $M900.2 million in the 1966-70 period. The proportion spent on drainage and irrigation and land development more than doubled in the second period when the total target expenditure of these two items was $M654.2 million. The social and economic effects of this massive expenditure have been felt in every Malay rural community. (See Mulliner 1969.)

12. Some squatters have been evicted in the Batu Gajah District. There are numbers of squatters on state land in the area around Ipoh, and also on state and private land in the Tapah District. In the latter district they are moved off when the land is wanted for building or mining.

13. Earlier development expenditure and policy has been succinctly dealt with by Robert Ho (1968) and Hamzah Sendut (1968). According to one district officer the objectives of the second Malaysia plan, which started in 1971, are to develop the economy generally and to change the structure of society in Malaysia by reducing the economic inequality between the wealthier Chinese and the poorer Malays.

14. Rents current in the Behrang Ulu area (southern Perak) for land under T.O.L. occupancy are: Padi or sago land M$7.50 per hectare per year; land for growing vegetables M$15 per hectare per year; tapioca land M$50-62 per hectare per year; house lots with no facilities M$10 per year; house lots with facilities (water and electricity) M$20 per year; shop sites M$40 per year.

15. The modus operandi of agricultural stations is illustrated by the agricultural station at Ayer Tawar, Perak. When this station was first opened in 1937 it was reputedly the best station in Malaysia and employed many labourers. In 1968 there were two labourers working 4 hectares. The equipment consisted of a disc plough and harrow and a tractor shared with another station. The station was developing *jambu batu*, a fruit variety introduced from Lucknow intended for local consumption but which could be used for jam making. It was first planted at the station in 1965, had yielded twice, but had not yet been planted locally. There was a *jambu* already planted in village gardens; but the new variety was larger and had less seed. Similar experiments were being carried out with a *limau manis* from Kelantan, mango and a budded *rambutan*. Fruit plants were sprayed at the station once a week and about ten local residents had been induced to buy a Japanese spray sold at M$12. The station ran a fruit rehabilitation scheme (*Renchangan Pemilehan Dusun*) aimed at substituting for the haphazard planting characteristics of Malay *dusun* the planting of half a hectare with a single crop. The owner cleared the land and dug the holes; the station supplied the trees and demonstrated the method of planting and husbandry. Since the end of 1965 about thirty farmers per annum have been supplied with free trees or plants. This station is being replaced by a new agricultural experiment station which is carrying out experiments with sugar cane, cocoa, tapioca, and rice. In addition there is an experimental cattle-rearing scheme at Ayer Tawar on 243 hectares.

16. The administration tries to encourage villagers to help themselves rather than depend upon handouts by linking the old practice of *gotong royong*, communal help for village members, to development projects such as creating a fishpond.

17. Competitions are held in the following fields: land utilization; health and cleanliness; *gotong royong*; cooperatives; adult education; community improvement; improvement of village economy. Prizes are presented at local agricultural shows, the members of committee of winning villages are sent on visits to other areas, and winning villages are given first priority when funds for projects are allocated.

18. It is said that, according to national land law, subdivision into parcels less than half a hectare is not allowed; and according to a law that is impending subdivision below one and one-fifth hectares will not be allowed.

19. This point is made also by Robert Ho (1970).

CHAPTER SIX: MANDAILING INVOLVEMENT IN MALAYSIAN AFFAIRS

1. Some modifications in this traditional pattern of distribution and growth were brought about during the Emergency when some villages were re-located and in the others houses were moved in to reduce the perimeter. Government-sponsored settlements and New Villages of the Emergency era have the pioneering square pattern with a few parallel main streets and minor streets at right angles, but the commonest form and the one to which villagers revert when left to organize themselves is ribbon development along road, path, or stream.

2. Six Mandailing patrilineal groups are recognized in this village: Hasibuan; Harahap; Mondang; Hutapuli; Roken; and SiEpeng. There is also a Bila household.

3. If it could be shown that this finding is generally true in West Malaysia then those Malaysian officials who wish to maintain the integrity of the village community along traditional lines would have in some way to stop villages from growing to more than about forty households.

4. In Lembah Keluang the dominant Tolu group supplies the headman who acts like a Mandailing *raja*.

5. The *imam* leads the prayers in the mosque and is often responsible for the organization of religious affairs such as the collection of religious tax, the administration of holy ground (*wakaf*) within the village, the maintenance of the mosque, and keeping the register of marriages.

6. In the Ulu Langat valley, ribbon development is common and the boundaries of villages are almost arbitrary; women seem to join the organization which best suits their constellation of kinship ties.

7. At Kg Gua Badak for example.

8. At the long-established Islamic school at Sungai Chinchin in which there are five classes, the basic curriculum includes: *Tauhid* (knowledge of God); *Tarich* (history of Muhammad); *Hadop* (conduct); and *Koran* (reading the Koran). Various aspects of *fiqh* (canon law) and *hadith* (the study of traditions) are progressively introduced. The building was erected by the Social Welfare department. A similar school at S. Lampam cost M$25,000; the pupils pay 50 cents (Malaysian) per month.

9. An accurate count was not made but my impression is that the ratio of boys to girls is about 3:2 in non-traditional villages and about 1:1 in rubber-dominated villages.

10. Half the children sent to secular secondary school came from one village (S. Bil); even if this village is left out of account, the number of children sent to secular secondary schools from the other traditional villages is as high as the number sent from non-traditional villages.

11. Trial emigration of young women from these villages is still at the rate of only 1 per 100 families.

12. I was told that the rice fields are worked at this village only when rubber prices are low.

13. Information about visits back to Sumatra before 1968 is available from nineteen villages.

14. In 1973 the air fare from Penang to Medan was about M$58 and the fare by sea from Penang to Belawan as a deck passenger about M$10. A number of visitors said that bus travel in Sumatra was cheap but uncomfortable.

15. Including a "private" visit to Chemor by the Indonesian Foreign Minister (Mr. Adam Malik) who is of Mandailing origin.

16. Malinowski used this assumption to explain different ideas among informants in a small social group. Robert Jay has recently attempted to relate different levels of generality in the conceptions of informants to the social distance between the informant and his topic and the formality of the speaker's relation to the fieldworker (Jay 1969). I have not been able to do the same in a systematic way but use Jay's ideas in the interpretation of my informants' statements.

17. The Bataks are well known in Indonesia as dog-eaters and pig-keepers whose heartland is the Lake Toba area in North Sumatra; almost all of them are now

Christian. The social system and language of the Mandailingers are similar to those of the Northern Bataks and were treated by Dutch ethnographers as part of the Batak culture complex (see for example, ter Haar 1948). In the 1920s there was a movement in Mandailing to deny that the Islamic Mandailingers and the Northern Bataks had a common origin. In contemporary Indonesia some Mandailingers recognize that their way of life and economic attitudes are similar to those of the Northern Bataks and they see the two groups as having political aims in common.

18. Proto-Malay forest-dwelling people.

CHAPTER SEVEN: MALAYANIZATION: PAST AND FUTURE

1. This framework I owe to Sjoberg and Nett (1968) who derive their ideas from Kish (1959).
2. Other migrants from Indonesia continued to come however. Dagli (1951) gives the following population figures for "the Malays":

1894	1,232,000	1931	1,962,000
1911	1,438,000	1941	2,277,000
1921	1,651,000	1947	2,514,000

He describes the increase in population from 1891 to 1947 as "fantastic" and says it cannot be accounted for by natural increase (the natural rate of increase in "old Malaya", i.e. Kelantan and Trengganu, is 1.5 per cent per annum), but as the figures show, the increase from 1911 onwards, taking into account base population, is not startlingly high by present Third World standards. However, the increase in Perak and Selangor to which many Indonesian migrants went was certainly very rapid.
3. The reasons why Pahang failed to attract Sumatran immigrants have been discussed by Cant (1965).
4. The two processes are illustrated in Leech's (1879) account of "Kampong Trolak" in the Selim river area: "A colony of trading Malays settled which has been here for the past four or five years; they came originally to collect gutta and other jungle produce and liking the look of the place, have settled permanently; these men, like most other foreign Malays in the peninsula, come from the Dutch Colonies and whatever else may be said of the Dutch rule in Malay countries, it appears to make traders and colonists of the people under its influence."
5. There is a procedure in Mandailing custom for the acceptance of a new member into an established village community. In contemporary Mandailing there is a small turnover of the village population and in some Mandailing communities in West Malaysia it was found that the turnover from 1963 to 1968 was as high as 10 per cent.
6. Soenarno (1960) divides the history of development of Malay political attitudes into three stages: a religious stage from 1906 to 1926; an economic and social stage from 1926 to 1932; and a political stage from then onwards. Some of the events of this period were: the founding in 1906 of *Al-Imam* "the first Malay newspaper that contained ideas of social change and politics"; the foundation of the first Malay political party, *Kesatuan Malay Singapura*, in Singapore in 1926; the development of Malay associations "all over the country" from 1937 onwards; the formation of a radical party, *Kesatuan Melayu Muda*, Malayan Youth Movement, in 1937; and the First Pan-Malayan Conference of Associations in Kuala Lumpur in 1939. The leaders of the Malayan Youth Movement were all first generation immigrants from Indonesia and, because the movement was anti-British, were interned in 1940. The movement re-emerged during the Japanese occupation under the name *Kesatuan Rayat Indonesia Semenanjong* (Union of Peninsular Indonesians) and adopted a red and white flag as a symbol of unity with Indonesia.
7. There were constant attempts (by the Chinese) to open up the administrative services to non-Malays. Mr. Tan Cheng-hock spoke on this theme in the Straits Settlements Legislative Council in 1925; in the Federated Malay States the non-Malay demand for entry into the civil service was rejected in 1935; and the Straits

Chinese British Association continued the agitation in the *Straits Times* from 1938 to 1940 (see Dass 1960).

8. G.C. Hart, writing in 1908, asserted that even in Kedah the Malays had abandoned every useful trade that formerly existed (quoted in Popenoe 1970, p.143).

9. The sponsors of the *Kesatuan Melayu Muda*, a Malay left-wing party formed in 1937, were all first generation immigrants from Indonesia (Soenarno, 1960). On the other hand Noone (1948), describing a Petani Malay village in northern Perak in which he carried out fieldwork in 1940, says: "Many inhabitants of the kampongs lived in a hazy world of their own which goes no further than the town on the main road." In Abdul Latif (1959) there is an illustration of a P.K.M.M. (*Parti Kebangsaan Melayu Melaya*, a Malay left-wing organization) procession in Malacca in 1947 carrying a banner which reads *Malaya-Indonesia Satu* (Malaya-Indonesia One) but we are not told from where the demonstrators came.

10. The value of education as a means of inducing a consciousness of nationhood has been questioned.

11. This period in the development of Malaysian education is dealt with by R.H.K. Wong (1965).

12. These included Dr. Burhanuddin Al-Helmy, and Dato Abu Hanifah bin Haji Abdul Ghani, president and vice-president respectively of P.M.I.P. (Pan Malayan Islamic Party) and Boestaman, a Socialist Front leader.

13. Malaysia was formed at the time from the four territories of Malaya, Singapore, Sarawak, and Sabah. Singapore withdrew in 1965.

14. It has been noted by the author that each village in Mandailing Sumatra has its own cultural features: in one village marriage by capture will be the norm, in another marriage by request. Each village has its own constellation of cultural elements. A conscious effort is made by the villagers to maintain homogeneity of culturally determined behaviour *within* the community. At elections it is common for all members of the community to vote the same way.

15. In one of these the headman has been succeeded recently by his son.

16. *Gemeinschaft* and *gesellschaft* refer to two ideal types of society, the former dominated by "warm", family-type social relationships, the latter by rationally organized relationships.

17. In contemporary Upper Mandailing the precept most often appealed to when deciding upon what course of action to take is the *biaso* (Mandailing language), the usual.

18. The statement "the new Malay immigrants from Sumatra intermarry freely with Malays already in the peninsula" (Vlieland 1934) is not true as far as the Mandailingers are concerned.

19. When carrying out the fieldwork for this study I was able to get information in any village about the two nearest Mandailing communities at least.

20. A Petani Malay who had been educated in Penang once said that in contrast to the traditional villagers at whom he scoffed he was a "modern Malay" who could eat eggs and bacon for breakfast.

21. McGee (1963) discusses, rather pessimistically, the possible role of Kuala Lumpur in the creation of a new Malayan culture. Spencer (1960) speaks of "a new kind of people here, *Malayans*, who may be of any race or ethnic mixture, who consider Malaya their home country, who think in terms of world culture and all the things that means, anywhere." Wikkramataleke (1964) describes "rural Malays" as belonging to a "dissociated" society which has yet to come to terms fully with the economic trends of the nineteenth and twentieth centuries.

22. I have seen an itinerant Mandailing merchant at a market in Yen District whose merchandise and mode of display were almost identical with what they would have been had he been trading in a market in Mandailing, Sumatra, though different from other local merchants in Yen. (See plate 7.)

23. In contemporary Mandailing, Sumatra, each family commonly grows wet or dry rice, rubber and, in Upper Mandailing, coffee, and cultivates a vegetable garden. There is also a wide variety of minor cash crops. Each family runs a miniature mixed farm, which is widely dispersed round the landscape. There are no crop specialists.

24. Leech (1879) gives some indication as to how this greater wealth came about: "I went down the river [the Selim river] to see the Kampongs and the jungle ... I saw a number of very flourishing kampongs and with one exception, on the left [East] bank of the river; these kampongs are situated on spots of high ground surrounded by stretches of wet padi land irrigated by a number of small streams flowing down from the hills to the east. The large majority of the inhabitants are foreign Malays, principally Mandelings, and their style of cultivation is certainly superior to that of the Malays in other parts of Perak, for which they reap their reward in the crops they get."

25. A few Mandailingers who have entered government service have continued to live in villages within busing distance of the capital, like Sungai Chinchin.

26. The social history of these communities has not been investigated.

27. At Ayer Tawar for example, Chinese farmers ploughed and planted some land intended as access lanes to land granted to local Malay villagers. In an area northeast of Chemor large areas of land have been occupied by illegal Chinese squatters.

28. In 1955 in Mandailing areas in Sumatra it was common to give enthusiastic welcome to religious teachers from outside the community. One or two well-known teachers were charismatic figures who staged a temporary religious revival in the community they visited and were paid for their services. There was a small number of Menangkabau men who came to Mandailing as traders, settled in the area, and were absorbed through marriage.

29. See Gullick 1958, especially chapter 3.

30. There are a few Chinese who have married Malay women and been converted to Islam. They live a Malay style life in Malay villages.

31. The vision that this seems to imply of all Chinese as wealthy entrepreneurs is false; there are poor Chinese farmers, fishermen, and squatters in West Malaysia.

32. *Highlights Second Malaysia Plan: Statement by the Prime Minister, Tun Haji Abdul Razak bin Hussein, May 27, 1971.* Kuala Lumpur, Ministry of Information.

33. In 1973-74 the villagers were asked if they knew of any Mandailinger in Malaysia who had become rich or famous, and the question was repeated with respect to Mandailingers from outside Malaysia. Responses were received from nineteen villages: Dato'Harun (chief minister for Selangor) was mentioned ten times, no other Mandailinger from Malaysia was mentioned more than twice, but the list included: a governor of Malacca; two former ambassadors, state councillors, the speaker of the Kedah parliament, the head of the police, two police inspectors, the commissioner for elections, the head of the cooperatives department, a customs controller, a high official of the Department of Education, a deputy commissioner of the Royal Malaysian Navy, an official of the Prime Minister's Department, a professor in the National University, the speaker and another member of the Perak parliament, three district officers or assistant district officers, and two wealthy merchants. Only two Mandailingers from outside Malaysia were known: Adam Malik, the Indonesian foreign minister who was mentioned eight times, and General Abdul Nasution who was mentioned four times.

34. In what have been called traditional communities on account of the system of social organization, traditional leadership and authority are still found.

35. In the Mandailing area of Sumatra the *rajas* effaced themselves during the Japanese occupation since they were seen by the Japanese as allies of the Dutch. However Mandailing village organization did not break down. As soon as the Japanese left, village governing councils were elected.

36. This system was sustained by the Dutch in Mandailing as a convenient administrative device, it rapidly broke down after World War II, was recreated by the Indonesian authorities in a new form after Independence but proved impossible to sustain and has disappeared in contemporary Mandailing.

37. It seems not unlikely that, if they had the choice, the Mandailingers would prefer a benevolent autocracy not unlike the present administrative system in Malaysia to parliamentary democracy. The latter is sustained by British-educated Malaysian intellectuals.

38. In an area in which oil palm had not been introduced, I met some criticism of the government in 1968, because it persisted with rubber planting.
39. This is characteristic also of the Mandailingers in Sumatra. Cooperatives there often last for only a few weeks and do a specific job or part of a job like sawing planks out of a particular tree. There are fewer cooperatives now in Upper Mandailing than there were in 1955 when a cooperatives officer was at work in the area.
40. It was also of course British policy to see the states as protectorates and to favour indigenous culture; Japanese policy therefore fortified an attitude that was already in the minds of Malay leaders.
41. For a more extended account of this period and its aftermath, see Victor Purcell (1967), chapters 14-15.
42. He is reflecting the British appreciation of the Malay cultural scene; to the administrator class, which Noone represented, dialectical differences were important because they affected communication with the people.
43. Popenoe (1970) deals with the *Bumiputra* congresses in the context of the development of Malay entrepreneurship.
44. The bases of ethnicity are well laid out by Enloe (1967).
45. Just how much Chinese and Indian feelings have been offended is unknown. The education policy of 1946 recognized vernacular primary schools; in the Barnes report of 1950 primary schools were seen as a means of building "Malay" nationalism; and the report of Dr. W.F. Fen and Dr. Wu Teh-Yu of 1951 pointed out the fear of the Chinese of cultural extinction. This fear must now be even stronger among some Chinese.
46. As we have seen, and as has been evident in Singapore for some time, younger Malays readily work for wages and soon adapt themselves to a monetized economic milieu.
47. Popenoe (1970) regards the working of tin mines by Chinese under arrangements with Malay chiefs and sultans around 1840 to 1860 as the first example of the so-called Ali-Baba business. If this were so then practically the whole of the West Malaysian industrial economy of the 1960s could be seen in the same light. My view is that the arrangements of 1840 to 1860 were like foreign investor-national government arrangements; Ali-Baba business refers to cover-ups intended to evade regulations.
48. It has been pointed out (Dagli 1951) that in Singapore, Chinese, Malay, and Indian workers have taken common action to enforce trade union rights in the past.
49. The concept of the New Malaysian is exceptionally well put by Y.B. Tan Sri Dato' Muhammad Ghazali bin Shafie, minister with special functions and minister for information, in a speech made in the parliament in introducing the Second Malaysia Plan on 2 August 1971 (Ministry of Information, Kuala Lumpur). Some Chinese intellectuals are conscious of being pushed towards conversion to Islam; and some Malay intellectuals have expressed to me the view that Islam would provide the best basis for a single community in Malaysia.
50. The attitude of the Malaysian government towards the Malayan Aborigines is perhaps indicative of what might be in view, as Carey (1970) says: "the policy of the Malaysian Government, at least in theory, is to encourage the *orang asli* (Malayan Aborigines) eventually to become part of the Malay community. This would seem to imply conversion to Islam." Popenoe (1970) states that a Malay lawyer said to him that he was most satisfied when hunting Chinese Communists. He expected a big blood bath or a "relatively bloodless take-over of full power by the Malays". This man claimed that his hostility towards the Chinese was shared by younger Malay intellectuals but it must be remembered that these opinions were expressed when the events of 1969 were fresh in everybody's mind and the present policy of the government had not been formulated.
51. Enloe's view in the late 1960s was that the immigrant communities would be willing to tolerate the special position of the Malays as long as their present rewards continued. This may still be so because the Malay show of political and military strength in the troubled 1969-70 period has made the Chinese retreat and increased their "tolerance" (Enloe 1967).

52. The difference between Perak and Selangor and to some extent Johore on the one hand and Kelantan, Trengganu, Kedah, and Negeri Sembilan on the other with respect to the ethnic composition of the population must be borne in mind.
53. Sweet rice (*pulut*) is essential for ceremonies; in Mandailing it is called the "glue of custom".
54. This is not so in contemporary Mandailing where lineage ties and ties to a wife-giving and mother-giving group affect the behaviour of individuals.
55. It has been estimated by Caldwell (1963) that urban areas will absorb over three-quarters of the population increase in West Malaysia between 1957 and 1982.

Bibliography

Abdul Latif bin Sahan. 1959. Political attitudes of the Malays, 1945-1953. B.A. thesis, University of Singapore.

Abdul Rahman Jalan. 1954. Tin mining in Selangor, 1874-95. B.A. thesis, University of Singapore.

Ahluwalia, Singh Satwant. 1970. Administration in Ulu Selangor District, West Malaysia. M.Soc.Sci. thesis, University of Singapore.

Ahmad bin Sa'adi. 1960. The development of Malaya's rice industry 1896-1921. B.A. thesis, University of Singapore.

Caldwell, J.C. 1963. Urban growth in Malaya, trends and implications. *Population Review* 7 (1).

Cant, R.G. 1965. Historical reasons for the retarded development of Pahang State, Eastern Malaysia. *New Zealand Geographer* 21 (1), April.

Carey, Iskandar. 1970. The religious problem among the Orang Asli. *Journal of the Malayan Branch of the Royal Asiatic Society* 43 (1), July.

Chai Hon-Chan. 1967. *The development of British Malaya 1896-1909.* 2nd ed. Kuala Lumpur: Oxford Univ. Press.

Cooke, E.M. 1961. *Rice cultivation in Malaya.* Singapore: Eastern Univ. Press.

Cowan, C.P. 1968. Continuity and change in the international history of maritime southeast Asia. *Journal of Southeast Asian History* 9 (1), March.

Dagli, Vadilal. 1951. The racial triangle in Malaya. M.A. thesis, University of California, Berkeley.

Dass, Danapaul Saveri. 1960-61. Malayanisation: Malayan Civil Service (1945-57). B.A. thesis, University of Singapore.

Ding Eing Tan Soo Hai. 1963. *The rice industry in Malaya 1920-40.* Singapore Studies on Borneo and Malaya, no. 2. Singapore: Malaya Publishing House.

Djamour, J. 1959. *Malay kinship and marriage in Singapore.* London: Univ. of London, Athlone Press.

Enloe, Cynthia Holden. 1967. Multi-ethnic politics, the case of Malaysia. Ph.D. thesis, University of California, Berkeley.

Fraser, Thomas J. 1960. *Rusembilan: a Malay fishing village in southern Thailand.* Ithaca, New York: Cornell University Press.

Freedman, Maurice. 1960. The growth of a plural society in Malaya. *Pacific Affairs* 33 (2), June.

Gullick, J.M. 1951. The Negeri Sembilan economy of the 1890's. *Journal of the Malayan Branch of the Royal Asiatic Society* 24 (1), February.

——— .1955. Kuala Lumpur 1880-95. *Journal of the Malayan Branch of the Royal Asiatic Society* 28 (4), March.

——— .1958. *Indigenous political systems of western Malaya.* London School of Economics Monographs on Social Anthropology, no. 17 London: Athlone Press.

——— .1960. *A history of Selangor 1742-1957.* Singapore: Eastern Univ. Press.

ter Haar, B. 1948. *Adat law in Indonesia,* ed. E. Adamson Hoebel and A. Arthur Schiller. New York: Institute of Pacific Relations.

Hale, A. 1885. On mines and miners in Kinta. *Journal of the Straits Branch of the Royal Asiatic Society* 16, December.

Hamzah Sendut. 1968. A new strategy for development. *Geographica* 4.

Ho, Robert. 1968. Malaysia. In *Developing countries of the world*, ed. S.P. Chatterjee. 21st International Geographical Congress, India, 1968. Calcutta: National Committee for Geography.

────. 1970. Land ownership and economic prospects of Malay peasants. *Modern Asian Studies* 4 (1).

Jackson, N.R. 1963. Changing patterns of employment in Malayan tin mining. *Journal of Southeast Asian History* 4 (2), September.

Jay, Robert R. 1969. *Javanese villagers: social relations in rural Modjokuto.* Cambridge, Massachusetts: M.I.T. Press.

Khoo Kay Kim. 1967. The western Malay states 1861-1873: the political effects of the growth of economic activities. M.A. thesis, University of Malaya.

Kish, Leslie. 1959. Some statistical problems in research design. *American Sociological Review* 24, June.

Leech, H.W.C. 1879. About Slim and Bernam. *Journal of the Straits Branch of the Royal Asiatic Society* 4, December.

McGee, T.G. 1963. The cultural role of cities: a case study of Kuala Lumpur. *Journal of Tropical Geography* 17.

Middlebrook, S.M. 1951. Yap Ah Loy. *Journal of the Malayan Branch of the Royal Asiatic Society* 24 (2), July.

Ministry of Information. *Highlights Second Malaysia Plan: 1971-5.* Kuala Lumpur.

────. *The New Malaysian.* Kuala Lumpur.

Moorhead, F.J. 1963. *A history of Malaya,* vol. 2. Kuala Lumpur: Longmans.

Mulliner, Brian Kent. 1969. Towards a silent revolution: rural development policy changes in West Malaysia. M.A. thesis, University of Illinois.

Neville, Warwick. 1966. Singapore: ethnic diversity and its implications. *Annals of the American Association of Geographers* 56 (2).

Noone, R.O. 1948. Notes on the kampong, compounds and houses of the Patani Malay village of Banggul Ara, in the Mukim of Batu Kurau, Northern Perak. *Journal of the Malayan Branch of the Royal Asiatic Society* 21 (1), April.

Ooi, Jin-Bee. 1963. *Land, people and economy in Malaya.* London: Longmans.

The piracy and slave trade of the Indian archipelago. *Journal of the Indian Archipelago and Eastern Asia* 3 (1849).

The piracy and slave trade of the Indian archipelago. *Journal of the Indian Archipelago and Eastern Asia* 4 (1850).

Pluvier, J.M. 1965. *Confrontations: a study in Indonesian politics.* London: Oxford Univ. Press.

Popenoe, Oliver. 1970. Malay entrepreneurs: an analysis of the social backgrounds, careers and attitudes of the leading Malay business men in Western Malaysia. Ph.D. thesis, London School of Economics.

Purcell, Victor. 1967. *The Chinese in Malaya.* London: Oxford Univ. Press.

Ramsay, A.B. 1956. Indonesians in Malaya. *Journal of the Malayan Branch of the Royal Asiatic Society* 29.

Schnitger, F.M. 1937. Archaeology of Hindu Sumatra. *Internationales Archiv für Ethnographie.* Supplement to vol. 35. Leiden: Brill.

Sharom Ahmat. 1970. The structure of the economy of Kedah, 1879-1905. *Journal of the Malayan Branch of the Royal Asiatic Society* 43 (2), December.

Sheppard, H.M. 1961. *Malayan forts.* Director of Museums, Federation of Malaya.

Simms, George. 1968. Malayan tin, a rich endowment. *Optima* 18 (2).

Sjoberg, Gideon, and Nett, Roger. 1968. *A methodology for social research.* New York: Harper and Row.

Soenarno, Radin. 1960. Malay nationalism, 1896-1941. *Journal of Southeast Asian History* 1 (1).

Spencer, J.E. 1960. The culture factor in "underdevelopment": the case of Malaya. In *Essays in geography and economic development*, ed. N. Ginsberg. University of Chicago Research Papers no. 62.

Swift, M. 1965. *Malay peasant society in Jelebu*. London: Univ. of London, Athlone Press.

Tan Sri Dato Muhammad Ghazali bin Shafie. 1971. *The New Malaysian*. Kuala Lumpur: Ministry of Information.

Tepper, E.L. 1965. The Malayan dispute in system perspective. M.A. thesis, the American University.

Tugby, D. 1959. The social function of *mahr* in Upper Mandailing, Sumatra. *American Anthropologist* 61 (4).

Tunku Shamsul Bahrin. 1967. The growth and distribution of the Indonesian population in Malaya. *Bijdragen tot de Taal-, Land- en Volkenkunde* 123 (2).

Vlieland, C.A. 1934. The population of the Malay Peninsula, a study in human migration. *Geographical Review* 24.

Voon Phin Keong. 1967. The rubber smallholding industry in Selangor, 1895-1920. *Journal of Tropical Geography* 24.

Wan Kalthom binti Wan Chik Bakar. 1970-71. Malay response to Confrontation. B.A. thesis, University of Malaya.

Wang Gungwu. 1961. A letter to Kuala Pilah, 1908. *Malaya in History* 6 (2), April.

Wang Gungwu, ed. 1965. *Malaysia: a survey*. London: Pall Mall Press.

Wikkramataleke, R. 1964. Variable ethnic attributes in Malayan rural land development. *Pacific Viewpoint* 5 (1), May.

Wilkinson, R.J. 1923. *A history of the Peninsula Malay*. Singapore: Kelly and Walsh.

Willer, T.J. 1849. The Battas of Mandheling and Pertibi. *Journal of the Indian Archipelago and Eastern Asia* 3 (5), May.

Wilson, Peter J. 1967. *A Malay village and Malaysia*. New Haven: H.R.A.F. Press.

Winstedt, R.O. 1934. A history of Selangor. *Journal of the Malayan Branch of the Royal Asiatic Society* 12 (3).

———. 1961. *The Malay magician*. London: Routledge and Kegan Paul.

Winstedt, R.O., and Wilkinson, R.J. 1934. A history of Perak. *Journal of the Malayan Branch of the Royal Asiatic Society* 12 (1).

Wong Lin Ken and Wong, C.S. 1960. Review article on *Chinese secret societies in Malaya*, by L.F. Comber (New York, J.J. Augustin, Inc., Publishers, 1959). *Journal of Southeast Asian History* 1 (1).

Wong, R.H.K. 1965. Education and problems of nationhood. In *Malaysia: a survey*, ed. Wang Gungwu. London: Pall Mall Press.

Zaharah binti Haji Mahmud. 1966. Change in a Malay sultanate: an historical geography of Kedah before 1939. M.A. thesis, University of Malaya.

———. 1970. The period and nature of "traditional" settlement in the Malay Peninsula. *Journal of the Malayan Branch of the Royal Asiatic Society* 43 (2), December.

Index

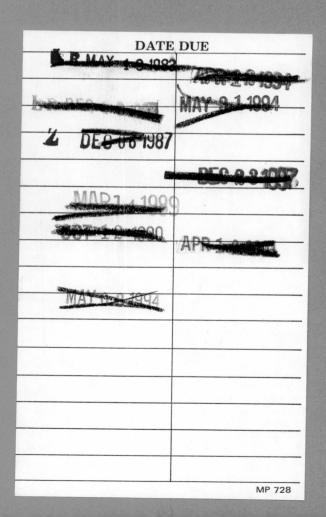